FUN-TASTIC ACTIVITIES

for Differentiating Comprehension Instruction
Grades 2–6

Sandra K. Athans & Denise Ashe Devine

INTERNATIONAL
Reading Association
800 BARKSDALE ROAD, PO BOX 8139
NEWARK, DE 19714-8139, USA
www.reading.org

The International Reading Association attempts, through its publications, to provide a forum for a wide spectrum of opinions on reading. This policy permits divergent viewpoints without implying the endorsement of the Association.

Executive Editor, Books   Corinne M. Mooney
Developmental Editor   Charlene M. Nichols
Developmental Editor   Tori Mello Bachman
Developmental Editor   Stacey L. Reid
Editorial Production Manager   Shannon T. Fortner
Design and Composition Manager   Anette Schuetz

Project Editors   Stacey L. Reid and Susanne Viscarra

Art   Cover Design, The Creative Shop; Cover Images, (red kids and top step) Shutterstock, (middle and bottom steps) Sandra K. Athans and Denise Ashe Devine; Interior Photography (pp. 3, 24), Sandra K. Athans and Denise Ashe Devine

The publisher would appreciate notification where errors occur so that they may be corrected in subsequent printings and/or editions.

Library of Congress Cataloging-in-Publication Data
Athans, Sandra K., 1958–
  Fun-tastic activities for differentiating comprehension instruction, grades 2–6 / by Sandra K. Athans and Denise Ashe Devine.
    p. cm.
  Includes bibliographical references and index.
  ISBN 978-0-87207-476-7 (alk. paper)
  1. Reading comprehension—Study and teaching (Elementary)—Activity programs.
2. Vocabulary—Study and teaching. (Elementary)—Activity Programs. 3. Literacy.
4. Interdisciplinary approach in education. I. Devine, Denise Ashe, 1967– II. Title.
  LB1573.7.A83 2010
  372.47—dc22

2009046571

We dedicate this book to our students, whose enthusiasm for learning inspires us; to our colleagues, whose passion and talent for teaching are essential to our work; to our administration, whose support and encouragement enable us to share our ideas with others; and to our families, whose endless love and understanding make this all possible. We are truly one part of a great team.

CONTENTS

ABOUT THE AUTHORS   vii

PREFACE   xi
Our Journey: The Development of Fun-tastic Literacy Bin Activities

CHAPTER 1   1
Motivating Students and Encouraging Independent Learning

CHAPTER 2   13
Getting Started With Literacy Bins

CHAPTER 3   41
Activities to Strengthen Comprehension Practice

CHAPTER 4   59
Activities to Build Vocabulary and Word Skills

CHAPTER 5   77
Activities to Construct Background Knowledge

CHAPTER 6   89
Activities to Develop Fluency

CHAPTER 7   105
Methods of Monitoring and Assessing Your Students' Literacy Bin Activities

CHAPTER 8   121
Literacy Bin Activities: Frequently Asked Questions

APPENDIX A   125
Reproducible Game Boards and Sample Directions

APPENDIX B   143
Reproducible Planning and Assessment Charts

REFERENCES   157

INDEX   163

ABOUT THE AUTHORS

**Sandra K. Athans** is a fourth-grade teacher and has provided instruction at this level for nine years within the Chittenango Central School District in Chittenango, New York, USA.

Having earned a Bachelor of Arts in English from the University of Michigan, Ann Arbor, USA, Sandra entered the field of publishing, working in New York City and White Plains, New York. She excelled in this field for nearly 10 years before pursuing a career in education. Sandra earned her Master of Arts in elementary education from Manhattanville College in Purchase, New York, in 2000 and her Secondary English Certification in 2004. She recently received National Board Certification in early and middle childhood literacy: reading language arts.

In addition to her teaching experience in the fourth grade, she has also taught at the preschool and sixth-grade levels and recently served as an adjunct professor within the English Department at Cazenovia College in Cazenovia, New York, where she provided reading and writing instruction.

Over the course of five years, Sandra also has been awarded more than 15 grants, the most recent being a Teacher as Researcher Grant from the International Reading Association for her classroom research. She is a frequently requested speaker on the topic of intermediate-level literacy and has presented at national and regional reading and writing conferences throughout the United States.

Sandra continues to introduce and provide instruction in many engaging after-school programs that encourage students' authentic reading and creative writing activities. She also champions her students' competitive writing interests and takes great pride in her students, whose work has received national accolades.

Sandra and her coauthor, Denise Ashe Devine, have published several books on their experiences studying and working with intermediate-level students in the areas of guided reading, reading comprehension, and motivation, including *Quality Comprehension: A Strategic Model of Reading Instruction Using Read-Along Guides, Grades 3–6* and

*Motivating Every Student in Literacy (Including the Highly Unmotivated!),
Grades 3–6*.

Sandra grew up in Westchester County, outside of New York City.

 **Denise Ashe Devine** received her Bachelor of
Science in elementary education in 1989 and her
Master of Science in reading from the State University
of New York–Oswego in Oswego, New York, USA, in
1993. She has been teaching for more than 19 years
and in that time has provided instruction for various
elementary grade levels within several school districts
in the central New York area. She is currently pursuing
National Board Certification in early and middle
childhood literacy: reading language arts.

In addition to this experience, Denise was involved in a summer
instructional program for at-risk students and their families. In this capacity,
she provided reading instruction for elementary-level students together
with their parents. Denise also serves as the fourth-grade chairperson on
the Chittenango Central School District's Educational Council Committee,
representing the concerns of all nine fourth-grade classroom teachers.

Over the past several years, she has actively been involved in
researching critical issues in education, such as guided reading,
comprehension, and motivation at the intermediate levels, and has been
awarded numerous grants on these topics.

In addition to these roles, Denise is an active after-school instructor,
offering creative programs in Readers Theatre, creative writing, and
vocabulary.

Denise is also a frequent speaker at conferences and workshops
throughout the United States. She and her coauthor, Sandra K. Athans,
have published several books on their experiences studying and working
with intermediate-level students in the areas of guided reading, reading
comprehension, and motivation, including *Quality Comprehension: A
Strategic Model of Reading Instruction Using Read-Along Guides, Grades
3–6* and *Motivating Every Student in Literacy (Including the Highly
Unmotivated!), Grades 3–6*.

Denise grew up in Liverpool, New York.

Author Information for Correspondence and Workshops

Sandra and Denise welcome questions and feedback from readers. Sandra can be reached at athanss@ccs.cnyric.org. Denise can be reached at devined@ccs.cnyric.org.

Our Journey:
The Development of Fun-tastic
Literacy Bin Activities

The literacy activities we share in this book evolved as a natural extension of the guided reading instruction we had in place in six of our district's fourth-grade classrooms. Our students eagerly embraced the activities, referring to them as "fun-tertaining" and "fun-tastic." Over time, we came to truly appreciate the significant contribution these kid-friendly activities had in reinforcing, extending, and supporting the instruction that took place in our classrooms. They also gave us differentiated avenues to help our students—exciting, creative avenues where we could do the following:

- Address multiple learning styles and preferences
- Use traditional methods as well as newer technologies for learning
- Encourage students' unique interpretation of the activities
- Support students' individuality
- Celebrate success for all students, despite the range in their skill and abilities

Today, we witness extraordinary events unfold in elementary-level classrooms across the U.S. where teachers have reshaped the ideas in this book for their own use, even though there may be some variation within the literacy instruction taking place.

Our Journey

The literacy activities we present herein are the result of a journey that initially began as a desire to help our students read better. For nearly

10 years, the dedicated group of classroom teachers and reading specialists we worked alongside were committed to helping our students improve their reading comprehension abilities, so every child could meet the rigors of the challenging intermediate-grade curriculum to the best of his or her abilities. The outcome of our collective efforts became known as the Quality Comprehension Model (Athans & Devine, 2008). It is an approach to strategy-based reading instruction that is best described through its four parts: (1) teacher-led instruction in the well-known comprehension strategies, such as questioning, visualizing, and synthesizing (e.g., Fountas & Pinnell, 2001; Harvey & Goudvis, 2000; Keene & Zimmermann, 2007; Strickland, Ganske, & Monroe, 2002); (2) the use of a Read-Along Guide, an innovative written component that supports the reading instruction; (3) independent student practice with the strategies; and (4) methods to monitor and assess student progress and skill development.

The model incorporates many of the best practices known in education today. Yet, it also includes a unique feature, the Read-Along Guide, which has often been referred to as the "missing link" by many who attend our workshops and professional development seminars. When using a Read-Along Guide, a student reads assigned passages from a leveled book and, within the multiple pages of a Guide, independently practices applying the comprehension strategies. (This process was earlier modeled by the teacher and practiced with assistance during small-group instruction.) Students are also often asked to write a response, enabling them to express views, ask questions, or comment on other issues as they engage in their reading. Additionally, students can review blurbs and examples appearing in the Guide that serve to remind them about the use of the strategy. Last, the students are also provided with prompts that guide their practice. A prompt can be directions, a graphic organizer, or the beginning of a key phrase that helps students apply a comprehension strategy.

Figure 1 features a reduced-size Read-Along Guide for Dalgliesh's *The Courage of Sarah Noble*. The cover of this Guide features the four strategies that the student will practice while reading this classic work of historical fiction: understanding sequence, recognizing cause and effect, making predictions, and finding meaning in context. On the first page of the Guide, the student is provided with a blurb describing each of the strategies, and on the subsequent pages, prompts guide the student practice. Through these multiple methods in which students demonstrate their understanding, or lack of understanding, teachers can easily monitor

Figure 1. Student's Completed Read-Along Guide for *The Courage of Sarah Noble*

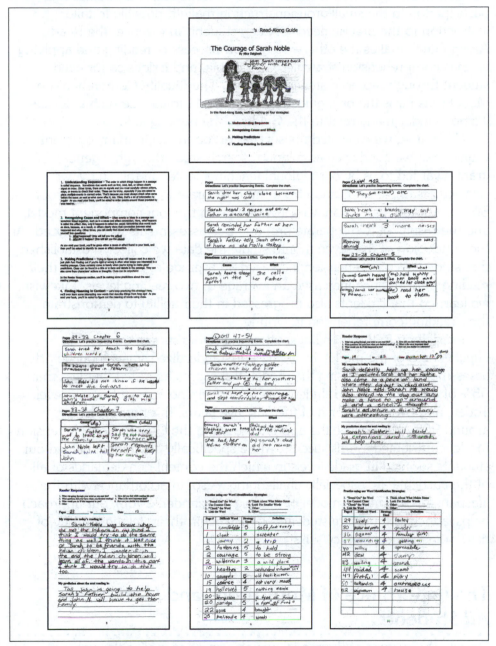

Note. From S.K. Athans & D.A. Devine, 2008, *Quality Comprehension: A Strategic Model of Reading Instruction Using Read-Along Guides, Grades 3–6*, Newark, DE: International Reading Association.

student progress, then confidently adjust their instruction as necessary. Further, the insights that teachers glean from the students' Guides and participation in the small-group instruction make it possible to tailor instruction to the precise needs of each student. In essence, the Read-Along Guide makes the otherwise unseen process of reading and applying various comprehension strategies very visible, and it does so for each student through repeated student practice. The Quality Comprehension Model thus far is the only guided reading model to include such a device— it's no wonder many refer to the Guide as the missing link.

Over time, we evaluated the success of the model in many different ways. First, we conducted an action research study through a generous grant awarded to us by our regional teaching center. In this study, we selected a sample population from three separate fourth-grade classrooms. Strategy-based instruction was provided using the four-component model, and the results of two separate pre- and postassessments were analyzed. At the conclusion of the seven-month study, the data we collected established that students' comprehension increased an average of 23.8%, while their reading performance increased an average of two reading levels. Likewise, we learned that students also progressed in their ability to demonstrate their reading comprehension in writing.

In addition to these findings, other indicators supported the effectiveness of the model, including our standardized state language arts assessments. Prior to using the model, test scores indicated that less than 65% of our fourth-grade students were performing at a proficiency level. Today, and over the course of the past five years, this number hovers around 90%. We believe the approach used in the Quality Comprehension Model contributed to this success. More specifically, the model helped our students succeed in grade levels in which the content-rich demands of all of the curricula are especially challenging. Also, in accordance with the lifespan developmental model of reading (Alexander, 2006), our approach helps launch and nurture students as they begin their lifelong journey of developing critical literacy skills.

The Importance of Motivation—and Motivating *All* Students

Despite the success of the model, we also came to realize through our action research study that motivation seemed to be a major factor affecting student progress with literacy. Although the link between motivation and literacy development had been established through earlier in-depth studies (e.g., Deci & Ryan, 1985; Guthrie & Wigfield, 1997; Lepper, 1988; Maehr, 1976), we were nonetheless alarmed to find that despite having a proven instructional model that helped nearly all students, there was a small number who did not benefit. When delving into our data further, the direct correlation between motivation and literacy learning was uncovered: It seemed that if a student did not participate during small-group instruction or practice applying the strategy in his or her Read-Along Guide, the student did not make the same gains as those students who did. Apparently, the members of this small group were not motivated in ways that paralleled the majority of their classmates.

Troubled by these findings, we considered ways to improve student motivation and effort so as to bring on board those students who, for a variety of reasons, were not engaged. Further, we also considered that even those students who were succeeding could benefit and be further motivated. Although we desperately wanted to tackle the challenge of students who were not engaged, we did not want to neglect the others, as is often the case. Challenging an already proficient reader seemed as suitable a task as aiding those who were struggling. As a result, we sought to identify ways of motivating *all* students no matter where their starting point was. We further decided that we should conduct research on our activities so that our conclusions would be based on data and could serve as a traceable starting point should we need to continue our research for any reason and at any given time. (This was, after all, an extension of our first action research study.) We were pleased to be awarded a second grant to conduct our classroom action research on student motivation and planned to address the following research questions:

- Could we affect student habits and behaviors?
- If so, which motivational strategies would be most effective in helping us develop the reading comprehension abilities of all students using our established model?

In preparing our study, we researched the activities of some motivational theorists (e.g., Ford, 1992; Gambrell, Palmer, Codling, & Mazzoni, 1996; Lavoie, 2007; Mendler, 2000; Sagor, 2003; Stix & Hrbek, 2006) and subsequently introduced numerous motivation-building devices that accompanied our instructional literacy model or were much broader and served to build student interest and engagement across the curriculum. Like the Quality Comprehension Model, our motivation improvement plan blended best practice as well as unique components. Among the new components we introduced to accompany our model was the use of "motivation bins," which contained activities that were originally described as "alternatives to worksheet practice" (Samblis, 2006, p. 693). At the time, our motivation bins contained what we considered *extension activities*, in that they were linked to our thematic reading units and represented an assortment of tasks. Students were not only given some degree of choice in selecting from among the activities but also were awarded prizes as they completed the activities.

Our intent in introducing the motivation bins was twofold: First, we hoped to encourage students to participate in the small-group instruction and independent practice prescribed in the model by providing them with an opportunity to work in the bins once they completed those tasks. In addition, we intended to entice them with motivation bin activities that were different, fun, and attractive, as they involved prizes (even though we recognized that reward systems did not meet with universal approval among educational and motivational experts).

In determining the outcome of our efforts, we collected qualitative and quantitative data: We tracked, tallied, and analyzed students' participation level, and through conversational student surveys, we obtained data on student interest levels. Finally, we conducted informal teacher interviews with those teachers who participated in our study. Based on the results of this research, the motivation bins were very effective and engaged students in unique ways that not only exceeded our expectations in terms of their popularity but also complemented our guided reading instruction. For example, teachers using the bins were surprised to find evidence of their use spreading into their small-group literacy discussions, journal entries, and end-unit assessment essays. Even the project-based assessments, such as their thematic teaching books (Harvey & Goudvis, 2000), included elements that came directly from activities that were included in the motivation bins. We were also able to document improvement in those students who were challenged by motivation and effort issues (Athans & Devine, 2009).

We were delighted with the success of these early motivation bins and began to share our early research at regional workshops and during our own professional development sessions. The excitement and enthusiasm expressed over activities in the bins was as unexpected from our peers and colleagues as it was when we first introduced them to students—and it kept growing!

More Than Motivating: The Creation of Fun-tastic Activities for Literacy Bins

As we came to understand the popularity, uniqueness, and powerful potential the motivation bin activities had as a learning device, we expanded our original thinking about their use for motivational purposes and considered ways we could maximize their effectiveness. Already having a tried-and-tested classroom model of reading instruction, we felt unrestricted in determining the direction we wished our bins to go. Likewise, we didn't need to keep our students occupied to allow the classroom teachers to meet with their small guided reading groups; our Read-Along Guide provided ample independent exercise, such as practice with the strategies, writing responses, and reading. As a matter of fact, we actually determined that whatever we were going to do with the bin activities, it must complement and not detract from the benefits of our students' work in their Guides. As such, the question we asked was, What more can we do to support our guided reading instruction and extend our students' skills and knowledge that may not be emphasized during our guided reading instruction?

To answer this question, we supplemented our existing collection of tasks with additional literacy activities that would target specific areas that we felt needed strengthening: building background knowledge, strengthening fluency, and providing more student practice with tricky comprehension strategies. We also wished to incorporate stronger methods of differentiation to allow for flexibility and a wide range of opportunities. Last, we determined that to maximize their already far-reaching motivational value, we would include activities that used electronics and technology, addressed a variety of multimodal learning styles, and were modeled after well-known games. Collectively, this was just the right complement we were looking for. Not only were we planning to maximize the use of the collection of activities as powerful learning tools, but we were also planning to do so with the best possible assortment and variety of activities we could thoughtfully, purposefully, and strategically assemble. As a package, it seemed ideal. As a result, our collection of activities soon extended beyond their original objectives. In turn, we began to apply the term *literacy* to the activities, because they addressed so many aspects of literacy in addition to motivation. Consequently, we began to call them *Literacy Bin Activities*, and we continue to use this term throughout this book.

Where We Are Today

Today, the activities in our Literacy Bins are aligned with thematic units of instruction and target the specific needs of all intermediate-grade learners. The activities do the following:

- Motivate students by integrating what current research informs us about varying learning styles
- Strengthen strategy-based instruction by applying it within informational, content area reading, which is often more challenging and requires a deeper level of critical reflection and analysis
- Build background knowledge urgently needed within grade levels where curriculum demands continue to escalate
- Develop student fluency, which greatly impacts comprehension and, at grade levels where independent silent reading is often stressed, enables teachers to address skill development in areas where difficulties may easily go undetected

In essence, Literacy Bin Activities are created to help intermediate-grade teachers address these questions:

- What comes next?
- What else will lead to significant improvement?
- Can we strengthen, extend, and keep our students moving forward as another component of our small-group, strategy-based guided reading instruction?

Use of the Literacy Bin Activities is the response. Additionally, the process by which students self-select and work on the Literacy Bin Activities (independently or in small, self-directed groups following their guided reading instruction) encourages and nurtures autonomous learning while also enabling classroom teachers to conduct multiple small-group lessons. Both remain vital.

Your Journey

We are certain that you will find some degree of constructive use for Literacy Bin Activities in your classroom. This is true no matter where you are with your reading instruction. It is also true even if you may be required to use certain materials for your instruction and if you may be working alone or with only a few colleagues (versus our six-plus). We are equally sure that your students will meet with success using the activities. No doubt your students will also find them engaging and will describe them as "fun-tastic."

Although we felt confident that our approach to our strategy-based reading instruction was successful and, for the most part, effective with students, you might not share these exact sentiments in terms of your own reading instruction. Still, this should not prevent you from trying out the Literacy Bin Activities. You may find ways to use them within your instruction that is different from ways described here. Likewise, you might find unique types of activities to include in your Literacy Bins that are dramatic departures from ideas presented.

We encourage you to explore, shape, and play with the ideas presented so that your Literacy Bin Activities reflect your style, serve your needs, and become your own. Considering that there is no prescribed path to follow, standardized design, or even a finish line at some universal spot somehow makes the adventure that much more engaging. Step right up!

How to Use This Book

We have organized the book into eight chapters. Chapter 1 provides guidelines that explain how you can shape the Literacy Bin Activities to motivate and engage students. The suggestions we offer are based on sound research, which we have also briefly described. Chapter 2 provides step-by-step guidance to get you started, and everything you need to launch your own use of Literacy Bin Activities is included. Chapters 3–6 provide numerous sample activities you can use in your Literacy Bins to target specific skills: Chapter 3 provides activities for strengthening comprehension practice, Chapter 4 for building vocabulary and word skills, Chapter 5 for constructing background knowledge, and Chapter 6 for developing fluency. You can use the activities as they appear, adapt them as you wish, or use them as models to create your own activities. Helpful resources are also suggested in these chapters.

Chapter 7 includes tried-and-tested classroom methods of monitoring and assessing your students' activities. Charts that can be used by students to self-select activities for their student portfolios are included, along with more formal grading rubrics that can be used for evaluating student progress and growth. Chapter 8 provides answers to some of the most frequently asked questions we receive during our workshops, as well as some of the more puzzling questions we struggled with while working with our own Literacy Bins. The two appendixes contain classroom-ready reproducibles: Appendix A comprises game boards and sample directions you can use or adapt as you like. Appendix B has other supplementary materials that will help you successfully integrate the use of Literacy Bin Activities in your classroom and assess your students' work with the activities.

Acknowledgments

We consider ourselves extremely lucky to have been surrounded by many supportive and enthusiastic people during the entire process of preparing this book. We are particularly thankful to the following people:

- The very skilled group of editors, production staff, and marketing mavericks at the International Reading Association, whose expertise helped guide us smoothly through another book-writing adventure

- Those theorists, authorities, pioneers, and practitioners who provided us with a solid foundation and encouraged us, through the simple act of sharing their expertise, to proceed in the right direction

- Our longtime friends at the Central New York Teaching Center who, over the course of numerous years, supported and encouraged our continued work in literacy improvement by awarding us with numerous grants
- Our colleagues, within our district and beyond, who enthusiastically participated in our studies and provided us with invaluable data, anecdotes, creative ideas, and information, and to whom we remain grateful
- The Chittenango Central School District, including our administrators and board members, who maintain their unwavering commitment to education as evidenced, in part, by their strong support for their teachers, and who have always cleared our path
- Finally, our readers

As we firmly believe, if you've picked up this book hoping to find some answers, a plan, or perhaps a little of both in your quest to improve student reading comprehension, we pass along these words to you in keeping with the spirit that enabled us to write it: *Use this as you wish!*

CHAPTER 1

Motivating Students and Encouraging Independent Learning

When planning an effective literacy curriculum for intermediate-grade learners, it is essential to incorporate activities that meet multiple instructional objectives. The reasons for this are clear:

- Rigorous standards continue to stretch students' skills in reading, writing, speaking, listening, viewing, and critical thinking.
- Steep demands to expand students' content knowledge in curriculum areas outside of the traditional language arts arena continue to grow.
- A broadened definition of literacy requires that students become adept at new skills to keep pace with advances in technology.

Although it is necessary to meet these challenges through the careful selection and mix of instructional activities you use in your classroom, it is not enough to merely have students participate—it is just as important to get your students to want to participate. As we are all aware, student "buy-in" greatly influences our effectiveness. Keeping this in mind, determining what will motivate students and sustain their engagement is critical. To this end, the literacy activities suggested throughout this book are created to help meet the challenges described above specifically by supporting your instructional practices. Here, they are designed to (a) supplement comprehension strategy practice, (b) build student background knowledge, (c) improve student fluency, and (d) strengthen your reading instruction while also promoting autonomous student learning. In addition, they are designed to pique your students' curiosity and sustain their interest, so students will want to complete them. The activities are differentiated in ways to address the varied learning styles of the students in your classroom.

In this chapter, you will learn more about why it is so important to offer activities that engage and motivate your intermediate-grade learners, while meeting important instructional objectives like the ones previously mentioned. Studies on motivation that are most applicable in terms of student engagement and productivity center on several theoretical frameworks: those that address the need for students to have choice and promote autonomy, those that discuss the diversity of student learning styles and preferences, and those that are linked to and support the research on differentiated instruction. Although these frameworks contain essential ideas that often overlap, each uniquely contributes to our understandings of ways in which we can better engage our students. By reviewing these essential ideas and discovering how they can be readily incorporated into the Literacy Bin Activities, it will become clear how to maximize the effectiveness of the literacy activities that you offer in your classroom. Also in this chapter, we discuss the use of "wow appeal," a playful term we apply to activities that are unique or that use electronics and technology—both big motivators for many students today.

What Are Literacy Bin Activities?

Literacy Bin Activities are fun and unique game-based activities created by teachers to target specific literacy skills while meeting other instructional objectives across the curriculum. In other words, the activities are thematic and tailored to coincide with the curriculum and the comprehension instruction that is taking place in the classroom. The activities are contained in a multiunit compartment, which we refer to as a Literacy Bin. For example, if a genre, such as tall tales, is the topic of the classroom reading instruction, then the Literacy Bin would most likely be a "Tall Tales Literacy Bin," and the activities contained within this Literacy Bin would make use of or align with some element of tall tales. Individual activities are contained in each of the separate compartments (see Figure 2 for a sample Literacy Bin in use). How do the teacher and students determine which activities will be used and when to use them? Students select activities using a popular tic-tac-toe game board; each square on the board features a different activity. Each student is given a tic-tac-toe board from which he or she will select activities, or they may be teacher directed.

An example of a tic-tac-toe game board for a unit on Colonial times appears in Figure 3 (a reproducible version of this figure can be found in Appendix A). Here, each of the nine squares briefly describes an activity

Figure 2. Students Using a Literacy Bin

Figure 3. Tic-Tac-Toe Game Board for Colonial Times Unit

Name: _____   Colonial Times   Tic-Tac-Toe

Vocabulary Activity	IT HAPPENED WHEN? TIMELINE ACTIVITY	Genius TV Talk Show! A scholarly showing of smarts (Library pass needed for filming)
Select one of the three word games from the sheet in the Literacy Bin: 1. Picture This 2. Poetry Vocabulary 3. Slap, Tap, & Snap Use the words from the "Colonial Times Vocabulary List" on that sheet to complete your activity.	Can you organize these important events into the correct chronological order? Use the dates as your guide. Look at the sequence of events that unfolds.	Our extremely intelligent student scholars will share their smarts about common questions on the Colonial period—live—on the popular talk show "Genius TV Talk Show." They've got smarts, they've got style…and just listen to them speak!
Colonial Leaders Hall of Fame!	READ Read at Home!	WHAT HAPPENED... AND WHY? CAUSE & EFFECT!
Create a portrait of a leader to hang in the Colonial Hall of Fame and include a paragraph about your leader's accomplishments. Select from: Henry Hudson, Peter Minuit, Peter Stuyvesant, John Peter Zenger, Elias Neau, Samuel Fraunces, General George Washington, Joseph Brant, Sagoyewatha, or George Clinton.	Have your parent sign your reading list of a minimum of five Colonial nonfiction books. My Prairie Year and Sarah, Plain and Tall are works of historical fiction. You can swap either of these in place of two nonfiction titles.	Use a cause-and-effect chart and find at least five examples in the book New York as a Dutch Colony and then five other examples in the book New York as an English Colony.
Drama!	Dare to Compare!	Colonial Sites
You will perform a one-person character play. Grab the spotlight and a book (Sarah Morton or Samuel Eaton) and tell your story (read it aloud) as if you were a pilgrim child growing up in 1627. Practice, practice, practice, and perhaps you'll get a chance to record your play!	Compare and contrast Colonial school days to today's school days. Read the article "Colonial Schools" and the book Colonial Teachers to help.	Visit some Colonial websites where you can learn more about this fascinating time in our history. Record five new facts you've learned, and let us know if you'd recommend this site to your classmates!

that is aligned with that time period. Likewise, the activities address one of the literacy objectives, as illustrated on the bottom of each game board piece. (The objectives do not appear on the students' boards.) Materials and detailed instructions to complete an activity make up the contents of each compartment in the Literacy Bin. The location of the activities within the Literacy Bin coincides with the numbered activities in the tic-tac-toe board grid. In keeping with the popular tic-tac-toe game, after students complete three activities in a horizontal, vertical, or diagonal row, they may receive a prize or some form of recognition. They are also able to receive additional prizes or recognition for each subsequent row of activities they complete.

The Power of Motivation

Today, we are mindful of the research that informs us that the way in which we provide instruction and engage students in learning experiences is just as important as the content (e.g., Gambrell, Morrow, & Pressley, 2007; Sagor, 2003; Tomlinson, 2004). For this reason, it is imperative that our literacy instruction reflect a variety of modalities that complement the diverse makeup of our classrooms. In the sections that follow, we discuss the connection between Literacy Bin Activities and research on student motivation that describes the importance of literacy instruction that gives students a choice, takes into account various student learning styles, and offers a differentiated approach.

Choice and Autonomy

Insights into students' reading motivation from pioneers such as Guthrie and Wigfield (1997) and Gambrell et al. (1996) clearly suggest that students engage more readily in literary tasks when they can exercise some degree of choice in the task. Encouraging involvement by providing many opportunities for students to exercise self-selection is a powerful feature of the Literacy Bin Activities. There are several options for students to choose from while working with the Literacy Bins: (a) activities, (b) books and materials, (c) collaborative peers, (d) the order in which they complete activities, and (e) recognition for their performance. (You will learn more about these options for self-selection in Chapter 2.) There may even be some degree of choice within the activities, which will become evident in Chapters 3–6.

Learning Styles and Preferences

Research drawing our attention to student learning styles and preferences has roots that date back to Jung (1927). Many models have since emerged that help contribute to our understanding of the diverse learning styles that exist among our students. Two of the widely recognized models that may help guide you while planning your Literacy Bin Activities are Gardner's multiple intelligences and van Klaveren and colleagues' visual-auditory-kinesthetic models (Gardner, 1983; van Klaveren et al., 2002). Although there are other models that address differences among learners, using these two to demonstrate how you might align activities to your students' diverse learning styles will serve as a useful guide.

Gardner's Multiple Intelligences Model. Introduced in 1983 in *Frames of Mind: The Theory of Multiple Intelligences,* Gardner's theory of multiple intelligences was based on his examination of numerous research studies undertaken from varied disciplines, including cognitive and developmental psychology, differential psychology, neurosciences, anthropology, and cultural studies. Based on this research, he identified multiple ways in which intelligence could be used to process information, solve problems, and create products of value (Gardner & Moran, 2006). In essence, he introduced the notion that there was not a single, universal way to define *intelligence*. As a result, teachers viewed students' skills and abilities differently. They also began to shape their instruction differently, expanding their parameters to embrace Gardner's multiple intelligences theory. Gardner proposes eight intelligences, although he continually assesses and refines his multiple intelligences theory: logical/mathematical, verbal/linguistic, visual/spatial, bodily/kinesthetic, musical, interpersonal, intrapersonal, and naturalist. Although Gardner is now considering a ninth intelligence, existentialism, he has yet to confirm this (Gardner & Moran, 2006). Characteristics of student strengths in each of the eight intelligence categories follow, along with suggestions for activities that would align well with each.

1. Logical/mathematical students demonstrate skill with numbers and logical thinking. Literacy Bin Activities could include student participation through numbers, calculations, mathematical situations, events, and functions.

2. Verbal/linguistic students have strong language skills and think in words. The activities could incorporate writing or speaking, such as crafting and presenting poetry or a persuasive essay.

3. Visual/spatial students command good visual/graphic skills and think in pictures. Literacy Bin Activities could include color, shapes, patterns, and other visually dominant components, such as a photographic essay or a collage.

4. Bodily/kinesthetic students use bodily movement expressively and think through touching and other physical actions. Movement or hands-on participation, such as pantomime or dance, could work well for these Literacy Bin Activities.

5. Musical students grasp music and rhythm well and think musically. Literacy Bin Activities could call for music or tonal patterns, such as creating a rap or metered poem or constructing a device to make music.

6. Interpersonal students are skilled in working with others and flourish in team activities. The activities could encourage collaborative partnerships in a variety of ways.

7. Intrapersonal students show a keen ability to self-reflect and are cognizant of their inner feelings. Focusing on inner states of being, self-recognition, and metacognition via a monologue, soliloquy, or self-reflective journal entry are suitable Literacy Bin Activities.

8. Naturalist students grasp natural events well and view their world through nature and environment-related schemes. Literacy Bin Activities could include collecting or identifying natural elements.

Gardner never prescribed specific instructional approaches or activities to align with his ideas on multiple intelligences. Still, the guidance he offers is to caution us against oversimplification, and he stresses the importance of recognizing and addressing differences among our students. By diversifying our educational approach so that we appeal to the range of our students' interests and strengths, we are better able to help all of our students learn (Gardner, 1999). If we present a student with a learning activity that is aligned with the student's learning style, we substantially increase the chances that the student will become engaged.

Table 1 features types of activities that could be used to address the different intelligences. Many are listed in more than one area, yet would reflect the unique contributions of each student's strengths and interests. As you plan your Literacy Bin Activities, you may want to review this list to ensure that your activities incorporate a range of learning styles.

The Visual-Auditory-Kinesthetic Model. Often referred to as the learning styles model (van Klaveren et al., 2002), the visual-auditory-kinesthetic model establishes three different types of learners:

- *Visual*—those who learn by viewing. Creating a poster or sharing information through a demonstration suits this learner.
- *Auditory*—those who learn by hearing and speaking. Performing a song, rap, or other oral activity aligns well for this learning style.
- *Kinesthetic*—those who learn through hands-on movement. Dance, crafting a model or sculpture, or activities that incorporate physical movement are appropriate.

There is some overlap between van Klaveren's visual-auditory-kinesthetic model and Gardner's multiple intelligences model. Therefore, if you subscribe to the visual-auditory-kinesthetic model, you could select from the visual/spatial, musical, and bodily/kinesthetic activities in Table 1. The same holds true for other learning models, such as the left/right brain hemispheres, the triarchic theory of human intelligence (Sternberg, 2000), and Lowry's true colors. Also, the Dunn and Dunn model suggests that students have preferences not only in their learning styles but also in their learning environment: sounds, light, time of day, and other variables. Although we might be limited in our ability to diversify all variables within this latter model, we can give considerations to those we feel we can diversify. Keeping diversification in mind and conscientiously creating activities that address multiple modalities will help you strengthen the attractiveness and effectiveness of your Literacy Bin Activities.

Table 1. Activities Targeting Multiple Intelligences

Logical/Mathematical	Verbal/Linguistic	Visual/Spatial	Bodily/Kinesthetic
Chart	Amendment	Acting	Animated activity
Collage	Bill	Animated movie	Dance competition
Collection	Canon (musical round)	Art gallery	Electronic activity
Commercial	Comic strip	Cartoon	Fitness activity
Computer program	Commercial	Clay sculpture	Food activity
Crossword puzzle	Debate	Collage	Hidden message/picture
Debate	Demonstration	Costume	Mosaic
Demonstration	Diary	Demonstration	Multimedia activity
Diagram with labels	Editorial	Display	Musical
Experiment	Fairy tale	Flipbook/zoetrope	Musical instrument
Food activity	Fiction story	Game	Needlework
Game	Finger play	Graph	Painting
Graph	Graphic organizer	Illustration	Pantomime
Hidden message/picture	Greeting card	iMovie	Papier-mâché
Hypothesis	Interview	Internet activity	Plaster of Paris project
Illustration with labels	Jingle	Mobile	Play
Law	Joke book	Mosaic	Poem
Manipulative activity	Journal	Multimedia presentation	Press conference
Map with labels	Law	Painting	Puppet show
Mathematical talent	Letter	Pantomime	Radio program
Maze	Letter to the editor	Papier-mâché	Role-play
Mobile	Linguistic talent	Photo essay	"Simon Says" game
Model	Newspaper story	Portrait	Television script
Number code	Nonfiction article	Prototype	Whole-class movement
Petition	Oral report	Rebus story	
Play	Oratorical competition	Slideshow	
Prototype	Pamphlet	SMART board activity	
Puzzle	Performance	Story cube	
Questionnaire	Persuasive letter	Television program	
Quiz show	Petition	Travel guide	
RAFT	Play		
Readers Theatre	Poem		
Recipe	Press conference		
Role-play	Radio program		
Secret code	RAFT		
Survey	Rap		
Timeline	Readers Theatre		
Trivia game	Recommendation		
	Riddle		
	Role-play		
	Science fiction story		
	Skit		
	Slogan		
	Soliloquy		
	Speech		
	Storytelling		
	Television program		
	Tongue twister		

Musical	Interpersonal	Intrapersonal	Naturalist
Animated song	Advertisement	Brainteaser	Animal expert demonstration
Anthem writing	Animated movie	Chart	Artifact collection
Audio recording	Choral reading	Collection	Classifying artifacts
Battle of the bands	Comic strip	Comic strip	Diorama
Canon (musical round)	Debate	Diary	Field study
Choral reading	Demonstration	Editorial essay	Fossil collection
GarageBand recording	Editorial newscast	Expert for a day	"Green" plan
Genre of music study	Fairy tale	Fairy tale	Habitat comparison
Historical study	Film game	Family tree	Insect collection
Instrument creation	Friendly competition	Journal	Interview
MP3 activity	Greeting card	Learning center	Leaf collection
Multimedia activity	Group project	Newscast	Nature scavenger hunt
Musical fairy tale	Interview	Performance	Nature tour guide
Musical poem	Maze	Poem	Nature walk
Odd instrument jam	Mime/charade game	Puzzle	Original song
RAFT	Museum exhibit	Reflection	Photo essay
Rap	Pamphlet	Research project	Rock collection
Riddles to music	Partner journal	Riddle maze challenge	Role-play
Singing finger play	Petition	Self-assessment	Scientific drawing
Singing instruction	Play	Short story	Scientific slideshow
Sound effects	Press conference	Timeline	Seed collection
Symbols for notes	Role-play		Sorting artifacts
Tunes over time	Survival game		Spelunking trip
	Team-building activity		Timeline
	Television program		
	Write a new law		

Differentiation

Tomlinson's work with differentiated instruction—"the craft of accommodating and building on students' individual learning needs" (Tomlinson, 2009)—helps us understand how to further refine our Literacy Bin Activities and maximize their motivational draw. According to her model, teachers can differentiate three things:

1. *The content (what is taught)*—Although many of us must adhere to state or national standards, we are nonetheless permitted some leeway. Literacy Bin Activities, which are often based on content-aligned themes, still afford us great flexibility to incorporate activities that approach the theme from multiple and diverse perspectives.

2. *The process (how it is taught)*—Over time, we all develop a variety of approaches and techniques that shape our instructional repertoire. A tremendous strength of the Literacy Bin Activities is that they enable us to easily introduce flexible grouping into our instructional processes. Interest-based groups, mixed-learning profile groups, random groups, and student-choice groups can easily be used with Literacy Bin Activities. This not only adds variety to our homogeneously grouped teacher-led reading groups but also ensures that we don't "pigeon-hole kids and end up with bluebirds and buzzards" (Tomlinson, 2009, p. 4). In other words, kids are not stuck in the same groups for extended periods of time; instead, we are able to encourage diversity and flexibility by changing our grouping structures with the Literacy Bin Activities.

3. *The product (ways students demonstrate their understandings of what is taught)*—The ways in which students can demonstrate their understandings using the Literacy Bin Activities is limitless and ranges from more traditional paper-and-pencil measures to new and creative outlets that represent new literacies (Kajder, 2006). Likewise, numerous ways to monitor and assess a student's understanding through formal and informal methods are also available for us to use with Literacy Bins (see Chapter 7). For example, some teachers encourage students to use self-reflective rubrics to consider their success with Literacy Bin Activities, whereas others rely on more formal assessment measures. Literacy Bin Activities allow for great flexibility.

Within these broad areas, Tomlinson further delineates that differentiation can be according to students' readiness, interests, and learning profiles. Clearly she reiterates the findings discussed earlier in this chapter that students' interests and learning profiles are key in planning and delivering effective, diversified instruction. However, student readiness in particular is a perspective that deserves special consideration while planning Literacy Bin Activities.

Student readiness is the factor often considered by many teachers to reflect the greatest disparity and thus the greatest challenge to address in their classrooms. Teacher concern over this disparity often outweighs concern for the range in student learning styles or interests. Still, the Literacy Bin Activities offer solutions to accommodate this. Many of the activities are impervious to this disparity in that they enable students to engage in learning experiences in ways that recognize and accept each student's unique needs and abilities. In addition, the activities inherently accommodate a diverse range of student skill and ability through the multiple ways in which students can exercise choice. They can choose activities, materials, and collaborators (see Chapter 2). Further, ways in which students are able to demonstrate proficiency is varied, and by working with Literacy Bins over time, students are able to demonstrate growth in the types of activities in which they engage, provided similar formats are used in multiple Literacy Bins.

Literacy Bin Activities provide great flexibility and can be used successfully to challenge and extend student learning just as readily as they can provide support and reinforcement to students who will benefit from further skill development.

Wow Appeal, Novelty, and the Rise of Technology

Literacy Bin Activities are motivating and engaging, as they easily accommodate and reflect best-practice findings as previously discussed. They can also deliver wow appeal and novelty in ways that complement your instructional literacy routines, which also have a definitive purpose and place in your classroom. Teachers who use Literacy Bin Activities in their classrooms continuously share stories of their students who clamor to learn of new activities or to search for familiar favorites, just as they relay anecdotes on activities that unleash new or hidden talents in their students.

These kinds of surprises present us with new opportunities to explore even better learning experiences for our students.

Literacy Bin Activities also enable us to explore meaningful ways to integrate technology in our classrooms. Activities can be directed to reinforce students' application of technology-based skills, such as keyboarding, Internet searching, blogging, and using multimedia. Likewise, activities can help students apply their skills to gain new understandings on theme-based topics through their use of these new literacies—Internet, visual, and others. Among their many strengths, Literacy Bin Activities can be shaped to help us establish a 21st-century astuteness in our students.

MOVING FORWARD

We must keep in mind two guiding principles as we strive to make efficient use of our Literacy Bin Activities by considering what research tells us. First, experts agree that no one fits purely into one category, which holds true for Gardner's multiple intelligences model just as readily as it does for Tomlinson's readiness factor. It is also commonly agreed that learning preferences are not stagnant but instead develop over time, just as a readiness level will fluctuate as a student develops new understandings and skills. As a result, we must exercise caution that we do not pigeonhole students into a single mode of instruction under the false belief that we are addressing that student's learning style or differentiating our instruction to meet the needs of a specific learner. As stated earlier, by varying our approach, we not only ensure that we reach and teach all learners but that we also address our responsibility as educators to help students develop multiple avenues of learning.

CHAPTER 2

Getting Started
With Literacy Bins

N ow that you have determined that you want to use Literacy
Bin Activities to motivate your students, build their background
knowledge, and improve their comprehension and fluency, what's
next? Where do you begin?

In this chapter, step-by-step guidelines show you how to easily and
immediately begin using Literacy Bin Activities in your classroom. You
will discover how to make your Literacy Bins, create game boards, and
locate materials. You will also learn how to fit these activities within the
larger framework of the literacy instruction you have already established,
as well as how to incorporate Literacy Bin Activities with thematic units.
In addition, helpful tips will also steer you through introducing students to
Literacy Bin Activities, determining how students might be instructed to
choose their activities, maximizing your classroom space and your time,
and selecting reward or recognition systems. At the end of the chapter, we
show you how to pull all of these start-up steps together and provide you
with a glimpse of what a Literacy Bin classroom actually looks like.

Using Literacy Bin Activities Within a Larger
Framework of Instruction
. . . .
Literacy Bin Activities are most effective when they are used within a larger
framework of literacy instruction and when they align with thematic topics
covered within your reading instruction. In other words, using the Literacy
Bin Activities to build background knowledge and supplement comprehension
instruction implies two things: (1) there is a specific topic upon which you wish
to build student background knowledge, and (2) you have provided instruction
on the use of comprehension skills or strategies, which you now wish to
reinforce through the students' participation in a selection of activities.

Another targeted area is fluency. Here, the objective is to provide an avenue for the instruction and practice of this critical component of literacy development that may not be emphasized during your small-group reading instruction. Last, enticing students with novel activities that represent dramatic departures—in format and scope—from the traditional pencil-and-paper practice may help to initiate a spark of interest in students who may demonstrate a reluctance or resistance to reading. For these students, the activities could be the gateway to literacy instruction.

In sum, coordinating your literacy instruction and use of the Literacy Bin Activities around the same theme (no matter how narrow or broad) is a way of unifying and rallying your students' efforts, energy, and focus. Additionally, this curricula double dosing inherently scaffolds students' understandings; knowledge is built as students progress between working with the Literacy Bin Activities and participating in the instruction. Moreover, this is accomplished in a unique way: through the blending of teacher-led small-group instruction and independent student adventure and exploration of the game-based literacy activities. As it will become clear, the Literacy Bin Activities are not busy work nor are they indiscriminant worksheets pulled together in haphazard fashion (although during your start-up phase it may at times seem so). Instead, they are carefully designed and selected activities that encourage skill development by either supplementing or enhancing instruction through differentiated instruction or a variety of learning styles.

Incorporating Literacy Bin Activities With Thematic Units

Literacy Bins rely on the use of activities that align in some manner to the same themes that are used within your reading instruction. Your themes may include those more traditionally associated with a language arts curriculum, such as biography, poetry, nonfiction, folktales, mystery, myths, or other well-known literary genres. Other language arts themes might revolve around concepts or ideas, such as friendship, bravery, challenge, coming of age, or even heroes, explorers, writers, and poets. All of these will work well for Literacy Bin themes. At first, it may take some stretching of the imagination to consider a variety of activities to align with the theme, yet in our experience this becomes second nature, especially when students are encouraged to offer ideas and suggestions (see Chapter 7).

Although both types of themes are typically used within reading instruction regardless of whether basal readers, trade publications, or classic works of fiction are used, you may also wish to use other content themes within your reading instruction. Reaching beyond the scope of your language arts curriculum specifically targets intermediate-level learners for whom a content-rich curriculum often proves challenging. For these young readers, learning new ways to broaden their critical reading skills across the curriculum can be a lofty undertaking. Some of the themes we have integrated into our language arts reading instruction include studies of Native Americans, Colonial times, the Revolutionary period and the New Nation, and immigration and the Erie Canal (see Appendix A for reproducible game boards used with these units). These themes fall within most states' fourth-grade social studies curriculum. We have also worked with talented and creative teachers who have designed literacy activities around science, math, and other themes (samples of their tic-tac-toe game boards appear in Appendix A). Some of the samples included in Appendix A have been used with students receiving special education services in grades 1–4, whereas others are used in classroom settings for grades 2–5. Common themes used for Literacy Bin Activities include plants, weather, communities, friendship, math, and word and language activities. Any theme or topic can easily become the focus of a Literacy Bin.

Covering content curriculum—including science, social studies, and even math—within literacy instruction continues to gain tremendous attention and support among educational and curriculum specialists, especially as the intermediate-level curricula grows robust as the result of many different factors, including the following:

- The No Child Left Behind regulations and mandates have resulted in the establishment of challenging standards-based curricula and assessments, all of which contain rigorous proficiency levels.

- The changes in technology and information sources have placed additional literacy demands on all readers and have cast fluidity on what constitutes an acceptable definition of literacy today (Leu, 2006).

- The indisputable fact exists that as time passes, there is simply more to learn.

Curricula double dosing may present your best chance of preparing your students for all the challenges that lie ahead, which we are incapable of conceiving today.

Although you are undoubtedly able to make a quick list of your tried-and-true reading units, you may wish to consider incorporating some themes from social studies or science into your units (if you have not already done so). Even if you do not teach these subject areas, the benefit of building student background knowledge and fluency using other subject areas as a resource is evident. Also, by reinforcing concepts that are learned in other curriculum areas, students' confidence is improved, as is their motivation (Paris & Oka, 1986; Schunk, 1985).

Table 2 features a list of themes that would be possible for instruction and use within thematic Literacy Bins. They span curricula and grade levels and even introduce popular trends and ideas designed to attract students

Table 2. Suggested Themes for Use With Literacy Bins

African American studies	Government	Planets/astronomy
Ancient history	Graphic novels	Plants
Artists	Habitats	Poetry
Author studies	Health	Presidents
Biography	Holidays	Rain forests
Butterflies	Human body	Revolutionary War
Civil War	Human rights	Rocks and minerals
Clocks/telling time	Immigration	Seasons
Communication	Insects	Simple machines
Communities	International relations	Spanish American War
Current events	Life cycles	Spiders
Dental health	Local history	Sports
Dinosaurs	Map skills	Tall tales
Elections	Measurement	Technology
Endangered species	Medieval times	Transportation
Explorers	Mystery	U.S. history
Fables	Native Americans	Water cycle
Fairy tales	Natural disasters	Weather
Fantasy	Nutrition	Whales
Figurative language	Ocean life	World history
Folk tales	Oceans/continents	World War I
Food	Olympics	World War II
Frogs	Penguins	
Geometry	Pirates	

in new and exciting ways. You may wish to blend some of these with your classic units of instruction.

Not only are the Literacy Bins theme-based but also all of the activities contained in each Bin in some way relate to that theme. For example, a quick review of Figure 3 in Chapter 1 clearly establishes that all nine activities in the Colonial times tic-tac-toe game board involve some element linked to Colonial times.

At first, it may be daunting to consider what kind of activities could be used for some of the themes discussed earlier or listed in Table 2. Still, there are many different Literacy Bin Activities that are surprisingly interchangeable across a broad range of themes. For example, you can see that some activities are repeated on a game board for the Revolutionary period and the New Nation (see Figure 4) and a game board for immigration and the Erie Canal (see Figure 5). For example, a "Word Search" activity appears in the same square on both boards, but the words

Figure 4. Tic-Tac-Toe Game Board for Revolutionary Period and New Nation Unit

Name: _____ The Revolutionary Period & the New Nation Tic-Tac-Toe		
Word Search **The Revolutionary Period** Find and highlight all of the words from the word bank. *Hurry! The British are coming!*	**What Are You Inferring?** Write some insightful captions and speech bubbles for these historical pictures and cartoons!	**NO TAXATION WITHOUT REPRESENTATION!** . We're looking for a new American Revolutionary Idol! Write a song or rap about this catchy phrase and perform in the competition!
COMIC BOOK WRITERS WANTED! Create and illustrate a mini comic book about your favorite event or battle from the Revolutionary War. Find a book in the bin for ideas. You may also choose an event during the formation of our New Nation.	READ Read at Home! Have your parent sign your reading list of a minimum of five Revolutionary War or government titles. *Buttons for General Washington* or *Secret Soldier* can be swapped for two books.	Are You Smarter Than a Fourth Grader? Read the book *Governing New York* and find some good facts and details that you can turn into questions. Get ready to stump your parents and friends.
Drama! (library pass needed) Try out these Readers Theatre scripts, "The Constitution of the United States" or "Patriots and Loyalists," or Genius TV Talk Show, back by popular demand. Hear our genius students share their knowledge on the Constitution!	Buddy Up & Create a Classroom Constitution What freedoms and rules do you think should be followed in our classroom? Pattern your constitution after America's. Be creative!	**Revolutionary Period & Government Websites** Visit some Revolutionary War and government websites to learn more about these interesting times in our history. Record five facts you've learned and let us know if you'd recommend this site to others.

Figure 5. Tic-Tac-Toe Game Board for Immigration and Erie Canal Unit

Name: _____   Immigration & the Erie Canal   Tic-Tac-Toe

Word Searches 🔍 **Immigration & the Erie Canal** Find and highlight all of the words from the word bank. Hurry, get ready to travel to new places and board new vessels!	**What's the Big Idea?!** Using a copy of **Kids Discover: Immigration**, select any three of these main articles: "A Nation of Immigrants," "The Immigrant Experience," "A New Wave," "It's the Law" and identify the big idea in each article.	**A Day in the Life of an Immigrant Child** Pretend you are an immigrant boy or girl and write a one-page (or more) diary entry about a day in your life. Read the diary aloud to another class.
Comic Book Writers Wanted! Create and illustrate a mini comic book about life on the Erie Canal. Be sure to include content vocabulary and illustrations.	🏠 Read at Home or to Third Graders at Recess! Have your parent sign your reading list of a minimum of five books on immigration and the Erie Canal. Choose from a selection on reserve at the library.	**LOW BRIDGE! EVERYBODY DOWN!** **Musicians & Song Writers Wanted!** Write a new verse for this popular canal song and perform it with your friends!
🎭 **Drama!** (library pass needed) Try out some of these Erie Canal Readers Theatre plays. You can find some friends who would like to read with you. Practice, practice, practice, and perhaps you'll get a chance to perform!	**The Art of Sequencing...** A Picture Game! On index cards, illustrate and provide captions for 7–10 events that many immigrants experienced as they passed through Ellis Island. Have a classmate try to put them in the correct sequence.	💻 **WEBSITES & VIRTUAL TOURS** Visit some of the immigration and Erie Canal websites in your Favorites folder. List at least five new facts you learn about each. Let us know if you'd recommend this site to others.

to search are obviously different. The outside or additional reading activity appears in the center square of each board, yet each is slightly different, having been mildly adapted to fit with the unique theme and the materials available. Likewise, each board includes a Drama activity, a Comic Book Writers Wanted activity, and a technology-based activity. You can decide how often you would like to repeat activity formats.

Chapters 3–6 provide specific types of activities that have been organized into chapters based on their primary objective: to strengthen comprehension strategy practice (Chapter 3), build vocabulary knowledge and word skill (Chapter 4; as vocabulary knowledge and word skill development are so strongly connected to all other objectives, a separate chapter has been devoted to them), construct background knowledge (Chapter 5), and develop fluency (Chapter 6). Also, integrated into each chapter are ways in which new technology may be included. Likewise, activity formats are designed to appeal to a variety of learning styles or address multimodalities. Although these activities are organized and discussed within this contextual framework, it is important to keep in mind that they can easily be adapted to themes other than those in which they are presented. For example, at many of our workshops, we feature a tic-tac-toe game board to align with a thematic unit called Meiosis and Mitosis for use in a seventh-grade science class. Although this subject is beyond the scope of our intermediate-level curriculum, we nonetheless easily adapted activities using a minimal amount of research and felt confident that pulling together materials to support the activities would not be a problem.

Making Your Bins, Creating Game Boards, and Locating Materials

The mix of activities you decide to include in your Literacy Bins must be given careful consideration. Ensuring that your activities reflect varied modalities, represent a range of learning preferences, and cover the scope of instructional objectives may seem intimidating at first. Based on our own experience and on our observations of other teachers who have adopted use of the Literacy Bins, the process quickly becomes manageable and actually enjoyable. This is especially true as you learn more about each of your students: their likes, strengths, learning preferences, and hidden talents.

Figure 6 features reduced-size game board grids with different mixes of Literacy Bin Activity types. Use these models as you consider a mix of activities for your tic-tac-toe boards. In addition to the concerns listed in the previous paragraph, two other considerations you will want to keep in mind are your students' needs as well as difficult content features of your themed Literacy Bin. For example, should a cluster of your students need practice with tricky comprehension strategies, you might want to include three or four comprehension activities on a game board. Similarly, one of your units may have many new vocabulary words, suggesting that three separate vocabulary activities on your game board might be appropriate. Creating the right mix, so your game board aligns with your students' needs and your curriculum, will also become a relatively simple task.

Appendix A features reproducible game boards that you can use and adapt to your needs as necessary. You may choose to work with these in a number of different ways. For example, you can use several of the game boards as they appear in Appendix A. We have included boards that feature

Figure 6. Game Board Grids Illustrating Different Mixes of Activity Types

A

Comprehension practice (Technology)	Fluency (Choral reading)	Comprehension practice (Verbal/linguistic)
Background knowledge (Verbal/linguistic)	Vocabulary and word skill (Musical)	Vocabulary and word skill (Interpersonal)
Fluency (Readers Theatre)	Comprehension practice (Visual/spatial)	Background knowledge (Technology)

B

Fluency (Technology)	Vocabulary and word skill (Visual/spatial)	Comprehension practice (Technology)
Comprehension practice (Verbal/linguistic)	Background knowledge (Musical)	Background knowledge (Read at home)
Vocabulary and word skill (Kinesthetic)	Fluency (Poetry)	Vocabulary and word skill (Auditory)

C

Background knowledge (Drama)	Vocabulary and word skill (Bodily/kinesthetic)	Fluency (Musical)
Fluency (Verbal/linguistic)	Comprehension (Logical/mathematical)	Background knowledge (Technology)
Background knowledge (Visual/spatial)	Fluency (Read-aloud performance)	Vocabulary and word skill (Naturalist)

common themes spanning grades 2–6, and within each game board, we have assembled a variety of mixed activities. If the themes coincide with those in your reading instruction, and if the activities align with objectives you feel are appropriate to address the needs of your students, then you may wish to use them as they appear (provided you have materials to support their use, which is discussed in the section that follows). They are also easy to alter should you wish to replace the activities in some of the squares.

Chapters 3–6 present multiple suggestions for activities, some of which may be better suited to your literacy objectives and your students' needs. Should you wish to create original activities, you can also use the blank tic-tac-toe grid provided in Appendix A to cut and paste activities as you choose. Many teachers are able to make their own Literacy Bin Activities using favorites they already include in their instruction or by reviving others that were filed away because of a lack of time. Although these activities might need modifications, so students can complete them independently, they could jump-start your efforts. Other teachers thrive on unleashing their creativity and welcome the chance to incorporate their unique ideas within the sound instructional structure of the Literacy Bins.

Although the task of making your first Literacy Bin initially may seem a bit intimidating, it's important to keep in mind that the process gets much easier with practice, especially if you are able to team up with one or more colleagues. Using a collaborative approach is a strategy we strongly recommend for many reasons: You can pool your resources to make it easier to locate materials; having the support of peers is encouraging and welcoming, especially when initiating a new project and outcomes are unknown; the workload for each team member is lessened as tasks are divvied up and shared among team members; and more importantly, having a "think tank" of ideas, insights, and problem-solving talent is an invaluable asset. Another point to keep in mind is that many teachers have found they come to share in their students' enthusiasm for the novelty and excitement the Literacy Bins generate and welcome the creative processes involved in making Literacy Bins. Keeping in mind that you can work slowly and build your collection of Literacy Bins from year to year will make the process less daunting. Additionally, once they are created, they can be used from year to year with few changes, if any. As such, the investment of time yields a product that has a classroom shelf life of numerous years.

As it will become clear in subsequent chapters, the activities that appear in the Literacy Bins are not leveled. Although the books that many teachers use within their small-group instruction are leveled (through any number of the common leveling systems, such as Pinnell and Fountas [2002]), the Literacy Bin Activities are designed to present students with another approach to learning. As a result, we have never considered leveling the activities. Instead, we encourage students' individuality and promote their unique interpretations of the activities. Allowing students to complete them to the best of their abilities aligns with the differentiated approach afforded by the Literacy Bin Activities. Additionally, we support peer partnerships (described later in this chapter), in which students work together to complete activities. Last, we also suggest that teachers may wish to help some students select appropriate activities (also discussed later in this chapter). As a result, although some of the Literacy Bin materials may be at levels that do not align with any given student's independent level—to which a student will comprehend the material independently with "95% or higher accuracy and excellent or satisfactory comprehension" (Fountas & Pinnell, 2008, p. 171)—these three methods alleviate concern for this. It is also important to keep in mind that the Literacy Bin Activities do not take the place of the teacher-led instruction in which leveled texts are used, but rather complements it.

Selecting Additional Materials for the Literacy Bin Compartments

In addition to the game boards, the use of Literacy Bins may require other materials, such as directions or samples, books and other reading materials, and art supplies. Although the tic-tac-toe boards include brief descriptions of the nine activities that students will participate in, you may need to provide additional directions for students, so they may work through the activities independently. Instructions can be succinct and comprise only a small note, such as the one in Figure 7, which is for an at-home reading activity. In this activity, students have chosen to take out books that have been placed on reserve at the library. The brief directions inform students to "use a Library Pass" to leave the classroom. They are also given the option of reading two

Figure 7. Example of Student Instructions for At-Home Reading Activity

Read at Home!

Please read a minimum of five nonfiction books on Colonial times at home. *My Prairie Year* and *Sarah, Plain and Tall* are works of historical fiction that you can read in place of two nonfiction titles. You may use a Library Pass and sign out an overnight book. All have been placed behind the desk. Our librarian, Miss Lily, will help you with this. (If you wish to read more, use the reverse side.) Have a parent sign your sheet.

Book title 1: _____

Book title 2: _____

Book title 3: _____

Book title 4: _____

Book title 5: _____

Parent's signature:_____

works of historical fiction in place of some of the other overnight selections, and to have their parents sign their reading sheet. (Details on working with others in your district, such as the school librarian, technology specialist, music teachers or others, are described later in this chapter.) Other directions might be longer, especially if they are part of the activity. For example, some of the fluency or background knowledge–building activities may include a script, such as the one featured in Figure 8 for the Genius TV Talk Show. In

Figure 8. Script for Genius TV Talk Show Activity

Name: _____   Date: _____

Genius TV Talk Show: George Washington & the Revolutionary Period

Directions: Select a passage from either *If You Lived at the Time of the American Revolution* or *If You Grew Up With George Washington* and turn it into a script for Genius TV Talk Show. One person will be a host, and there can be up to three different genius student speakers. The host can take turns with a speaker, so everyone can be a genius! Perform in front of your class and remember to read punctuation, speak clearly, and watch your pacing (not too fast or too slow)!

Setting: The television host sits in a chair behind a desk while student speakers are in chairs surrounding the host.

Host: (*speak to classroom audience*) "Surely you have questions about what life was like back in the days of George Washington during the Revolutionary period in our history. Today we've invited some extremely intelligent student scholars to present information on these eventful times. I'd like to introduce myself as the host of Genius TV Talk Show! My name is (*host's fictitious name*), and my first guest speaker today is the super smart, extremely intelligent (*speaker 1's fictitious name*). The question we will be asking (*speaker 1's fictitious name*) is (*read question from book*). Now, why don't you share your insights on the answer to this question!"

Speaker 1:   (*read from the passage in the text while the host and other speakers listen, read the punctuation, and watch your fluency*)

Host: "Thanks for sharing those genius insights! Let's have a round of applause for our speaker, (*speaker 1's fictitious name*)."

Speaker 1:   "It was my pleasure!" (*stand, take a bow, and sit down*)

Host: "Our next speaker is the brilliant and exceptionally keen-minded (*speaker 2's fictitious name*). The question we will be asking (*speaker 2's fictitious name*) is (*read question from book*). Now, why don't you share your insights on the answer to this question!"

Speaker 2:   (*read from the passage in the text while the host and other speakers listen, read the punctuation, and watch your fluency*)

Continue in this manner until all speakers have had a turn.

this activity, students use a generic script that includes italicized areas where passages of informational text may be inserted. The script is included in the compartment for that activity (Appendix A includes other sample directions).

Books and any other reading materials that are required for students to independently complete an activity should also be included in the compartments or in an easily accessible area. Often, many teachers use a separate container, referred to as the Literacy Bin Library or even a basket, which includes a variety of books, magazines, and other reading materials. All are aligned to the theme and can be used interchangeably for a number of Literacy Bin Activities (see Figure 9). Figure 10 contains directions for an activity that makes use of materials contained in a Literacy Bin Library. As is evident from the example, students can select from a variety of books or literature from the Literacy Bin Library to complete the tall tale activity. In other cases, specific titles might be included within an activity compartment. Some teachers have also reserved books in the library, so students from different classrooms can use them.

Art materials need not be highly sophisticated, complicated, or in need of much cleanup time. We often include only basic materials, such as construction paper, and show students where they can locate glue, markers,

Figure 9. Literacy Bin Library

Figure 10. Directions for an Activity Using Literacy Bin Library Materials

Name: _____ Date: _____

Comic Book Writer & Illustrator *Wanted*!

Directions: For this activity, select one of the exciting tall tales from the Literacy Bin Library and enjoy reading the adventures of a larger-than-life character. Then, write and illustrate a seven-page comic book about the tale.

Be sure to:
1. Break down the tale into seven main episodes.
2. Write speech bubbles or narrate the episodes. (Watch your spelling.)
3. Include colorful illustrations.
4. Attach a cover to your comic book and include your name at the bottom.

---

crayons, scissors, and other supplies that are needed. Informing students of the whereabouts of art supplies can take place at the time the Literacy Bins are introduced. If necessary, this can be reinforced during the introduction of each subsequent Literacy Bin. Establishing one storage area, such as a cabinet, crate, shelf, or window ledge, where students can locate all of the materials they might need may be something you will wish to consider to support the students' independence as they work with the Literacy Bin Activities.

Introducing Students to Literacy Bin Activities

Establishing some procedures when Literacy Bins are first introduced into your classroom will help clarify the roles and responsibilities students need to assume to make the Literacy Bin Activities work effectively. Creating courtesy tips (Guastello & Lenz, 2007) or "Read-iquette Reminders" that specify behaviors that allow both the small-group instruction and the Literacy Bin Activities to take place simultaneously may be helpful. As an example, we coined this playful term *read-iquette* as a variation of the word *etiquette* and brainstormed the following behavior guidelines with our students:

• Please use whisper voices.

• Quietly troubleshoot problems with a friend.

• Please don't disturb group lessons.

- Work cooperatively.
- Return materials to the proper place.

These guidelines worked very well. Students easily adopted the behaviors and also recognized the importance of being considerate of others.

Literacy Bin Activities are designed to be used individually by students or in small self-directed teams of 2–5 students. To begin, you may wish to distribute a tic-tac-toe game board to all students and display a Literacy Bin containing the activities and materials. Then, you may want to explain the Literacy Bin and the Literacy Bin Activities contained inside, describing their connection to the students' tic-tac-toe boards and sharing some of the activities. Explaining how the grids on the tic-tac-toe boards align with the numbering system on the Literacy Bin will ensure that students can easily locate materials. You may also want to explain how and when the Literacy Bin Activities are used, review all activities with materials, and share your expectations about the quality of the work. "A quick-check" guideline (discussed in Chapter 7) provides helpful tips on devising a classroom set of expectations. Briefly, the phrase reminds students that during the teacher's quick check of a completed activity, he or she will be looking for accuracy, quality work, and complete work, words that begin with the same letters of "a quick check." You may also want to share your monitoring and assessment practices and distribute any devices related to them. Many options are provided for you in Chapter 7.

You may find the following script helpful for introducing the activities to your students:

....

I know you're all wondering what's in this big box. It contains what many former students call "fun–tastic activities." There's drama, comic book writing, poetry, computer tasks, drawing, and more!

Take a look at your tic-tac-toe game board, and you'll see a short description of the fun–tastic activities in this bin. There is also a number on your game board that corresponds to a numbered compartment in the bin. This lets you quickly find the materials for the activity you want to complete. Let's take a look at some of them (*pause and read two or three*). All materials you'll need for the activities are in the Literacy Bin compartments. When you complete three activities in a row, you'll receive (*share your reward or recognition system*).

As you can tell from your game board, this Literacy Bin is all about *theme*, so all of the activities have to do with *theme*. The way it works is, when you've completed your reading assignments from our small-group instruction, you can work on these activities.

Now, let's take some time and take a closer look at all of the activities. *(You may wish to review all activities and materials, discuss where art materials will be located, and review unique features of specific activities, such as the use of a Library or other pass, Literacy Bin Library, etc.)* I'd like to take a look at your completed activities frequency. *(You may wish to check them every Friday, after every two activities, at the end of instruction daily, etc.)*

Let's now talk about expectations, but instead of telling you what I expect, we're going to do this together. *(Should you decide to adopt the expectations we call "a quick check" for accuracy, quality work, and complete work as described in Chapter 7, you may wish to explain them here. As an alternative, you might wish to have students participate in a group activity to create your own classroom expectations. Following this activity, you might also share your monitoring and assessment methods.)*

We're going to begin working with the Literacy Bin Activities tomorrow.

....

Once students have been introduced to the Literacy Bin Activities, they should be able to work on them independently or in a small group without further explanation or assistance. As you will be working with reading groups simultaneously, you will likely be unable to assist students working on Literacy Bin Activities. Although students may need some time to make the transition into this process, in our experience it quickly becomes routine.

Selecting Literacy Bin Activities: Student Choice and Autonomy

The tic-tac-toe grid is an easy system for students to grasp, and it takes little explanation even when you first introduce the Literacy Bin Activities in your classroom. Interestingly, most students approach their selection process with the intent to win a tic-tac-toe by completing three activities in a row. However, there are students who instead select activities that seem interesting, challenging, or aligned to their interests, such as drawing or musical activities. In keeping with the flexible nature of the Literacy Bin Activities, teachers may choose to work with the activity selection process in any number of ways, which are described in the next section.

Students Choose All Activities

Knowing that most students will work toward completing three activities in a row, teachers may want to vary the activities and strategically place them on the game board so that students participate in a variety of different activities. Students may also choose activities that they know they will enjoy, they might seek a challenge or pick ones that will enable them to explore new experiences, or they may pick some to help strengthen a skill. Although students use unique criteria when making their selection, all are perfectly acceptable and work well. Even if you unintentionally encourage student selection through the placement of activities in a game board or when directing some of the selection process, you still might wish to provide students with the opportunity to self-select some of the activities to make use of this very powerful motivating force.

Self-selection can aid students in developing independent, autonomous work skills. Although there are few who would debate the importance of students developing the ability to work and function independently, this skill may not be one that is regularly taught through direct instruction and practiced. Instead, self-selection often seems to be expected, an inherent outcome from the natural progression students make as they move from one grade level to the next. Still, this may not happen succinctly for all students. As an example, new challenges may pose minor difficulties for some students, and skills that previously helped them may now prove unreliable. Using the Literacy Bin Activities as a way to develop, support, and enhance this independence is another avenue that teachers may wish to address as they integrate the Literacy Bin Activities into their classrooms.

We have also encountered some students who initially had trouble determining which activities to choose, a dilemma we had not anticipated, especially in consideration of the resounding research over the importance of choice as a motivating factor. Still, as we evaluated the number of activities students completed during our classroom research, we found that some struggled greatly with selecting activities. Some spent too much time overthinking the selection process to the point of accomplishing very little,

Figure 11. Suggestions to Help Students Make Activity Selections

Having Trouble Picking an Activity?

Here are some things to try:
 1. Select an activity that sounds fun or interesting.
 2. Choose an activity that you've never tried before.
 3. Pick an activity that will help you strengthen a skill.
 4. Ask a friend which activity he or she liked best.
 5. Is there an activity you want to work on with a family member at home?
 6. Maybe you should try an activity you can do with a small group of friends?
 7. Have you chosen an activity you can do all by yourself?
 8. Are there special art materials you'd like to work with?
 9. Can you use your musical instrument in an activity?
10. Will certain activities help you get a tic-tac-toe?
11. Do you have other special talents you can use in an activity?
12. Do you collect anything you could use as a prop in an activity?
13. Did you enjoy watching an activity your classmates performed?
14. Eenie, meenie, miny, moe!
15. Try out each one of these ideas in order.

Remember, it's also important to stick with an activity. Always complete one before you begin another!

or they started and then discarded one activity after another without ever finishing them. Upon further investigation, we learned that these students had little practice developing strategies to choose activities and consider ways in which to make good selections. Providing some lessons in this may be advantageous for some students and might best be reviewed with students as you introduce the Literacy Bins within your classroom. Figure 11 presents some helpful suggestion for students as they consider ways in which to make activity selections.

Teachers Suggest All Activities

As teachers work closely with students during small-group instructional time, as well as at other times during the school day, individual students' literacy needs become very clear. Teachers wishing to encourage students to build fluency or background knowledge, or to practice strategies, may suggest activities to students by highlighting them with a marker or placing a sticker on the grid on a student's game board. Although both methods work well in helping struggling readers build targeted skills, these methods can also be used to extend and challenge proficient readers. Teachers may also wish to steer some students toward activities to help build their self-esteem and confidence or to encourage their success. As the Literacy Bin Activities are not leveled, some students may benefit from teacher guidance.

Students Choose Some Activities

You may suggest that some activities be completed first by some students and then encourage self-selection if time permits. This approach represents the happy medium that many teachers eventually adopt; it ensures that students build skills that may need strengthening prior to participating in other activities. Helping students prioritize their efforts (and discussing this plan with them) is critical to maximizing the effectiveness of the Literacy Bins.

Students Design an Activity

Another approach is to allow students to exchange a square for an activity of their devising. Those students who thrive on challenge and demonstrate proficiency in literacy skills may have some ideas of their own, just as some students who struggle with particular skills may have exciting suggestions on how they can direct their own skill development. Allowing this kind of creative self-directed study can easily be accommodated in the game board by enabling students to replace a square with an activity they've created. Teachers using this approach have typically requested that a brief description be submitted by the student for a "swap out" and that only one is allowed per game board. A swap-out card, which resembles a square in a tic-tac-toe grid (only larger), is featured in Figure 12. Keeping in mind that the process of working with the Literacy Bins should support student independence as another benefit of using them in intermediate-level classrooms, the process cannot be undermined by another built-in process that requires teacher consideration and approval. In our experience, this system has worked very well and has many positive benefits without becoming cumbersome to administer.

Figure 12. Swap-Out Card

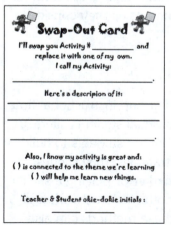

Students Choose Collaborative Peers

Although many Literacy Bin Activities are intended to be completed by students independently, you may decide to have students work collaboratively in pairs or in larger groups for several reasons. Enabling students to work together can be very motivating to some students, especially for those who may not get the chance to work together often. Also, taking advantage of beneficial partnering by pairing students who contribute different strengths to a task can help motivate students to stick to challenging tasks by encouraging them to support (and learn from) each other. If teachers can involve colleagues and other school professionals, such as the librarian or media specialist, for some of their Literacy Bin Activities, students may also be offered the option to choose to work with these other adults. This type of collaboration may also be motivating to some students. The concept of flexible grouping is discussed later in this chapter.

Students Choose the Order to Complete Activities

Students can select the order in which they want to complete activities, and although teachers may encourage the order of activities through their placement in a tic-tac-toe or game board, students still have a great deal of choice in determining which activities they wish to complete first. This type of choice sustains students' interest and encourages them to complete numerous activities within a Literacy Bin.

Classroom Space, Location, and Time

Rather than have a stationary work space, Literacy Bin Activities are designed to be used at a student's desk or in any small area that is not being used. We have found that many teachers we work with do not have an abundance of space and cannot designate permanent work stations for Literacy Bin Activities. The only space needed for use of the Literacy Bins is an easily accessible area to house the bin of materials.

You might also consider using areas outside of your classroom. Of course, this should only be done if these locations are supervised. For example, we often sent small groups of students to the library, music rooms, the computer lab, and even to other classrooms to practice plays or musical activities or to work in small teams or independently with another adult. Planning in advance for the use of these additional spaces will help make this type of movement routine and therefore not take you away from your small-group instruction. Including passes to the other locations within the compartments of the Literacy Bins and, if need be, using sign-up sheets should multiple students wish to go to the same space, such as the school library, will build this process into the use of the Literacy Bins. Discussing schedules, expectations, behavior, and other matters must be worked out in advance with students as well as with those teaching professionals in other locations who wish to participate in your Literacy Bin Activities. However, in our experience, we rarely encountered difficulties and instead were very pleased by the tremendous support and enthusiasm that our librarian, music teachers, and others expressed, demonstrated, and even touted while supervising or assisting students with their activities.

As the Literacy Bins are designed to be used alongside your reading instruction, the length of time that a Literacy Bin is used depends largely on the length of time of your instructional reading unit. Most of our instructional units last 1–2 weeks. However, we often have some type of formal assessment that follows (Athans & Devine, 2008). These might be project based, such as creating a classroom quilt for which each student contributes a square involving reading, research, and writing. Others might be more traditional and follow the format used in our standardized state tests, which include multiple-choice questions, short-answer and extended-response questions, and an essay. As such, this may add two or more days to each unit. Additionally, our small-group guided reading instruction is a component of a much larger balanced literacy umbrella that includes activities such as read-alouds, independent reading, and literature circles. Therefore, we might continue working in the Literacy Bin as an instructional unit ends and the class begins a read-aloud.

Some of the Literacy Bins we have used actually contain two themes, as demonstrated in Figure 4, that cover the Revolutionary period and the New Nation. Many teachers used this Literacy Bin for up to six weeks as students worked through these two related themes. Figure 5 is another tic-tac-toe game board in which two themes are featured, immigration and the Erie Canal. This Literacy Bin was also used for a period beyond one instructional reading unit.

You may consider starting off by introducing one or two Literacy Bins in the first year and building onto your collection in subsequent years.

Also, determining how long you would like to continue keeping a Literacy Bin in use may be determined by the number of activities that students are able to complete. In some cases, we had little time for Literacy Bin Activities, and students asked that they be able to continue working through the activities despite moving on to a read-aloud or other literacy activities.

Although the use of rewards such as prizes remains a topic of debate (Willingham, 2007), we have found that many intermediate-level students are motivated by the opportunity to receive a prize. As such, we have always included them within our Literacy Bin Activities practices. Additionally, the game concept that forms the superstructure of the Literacy Bins seems to suggest that there is an element not only of playing but of winning as well. For these reasons, we continue to offer a variety of inexpensive prizes. If you are uncomfortable with prizes, you may consider awarding points, earning stickers, or having the students place their names on a "wall of fame." You are the person best suited to determine whether prizes or recognition rewards are used.

Many teachers who use a reward or recognition system in their classroom also provide students with choices. For example, a student might choose a favorite sticker from among a selection of five different designs. Alternatively, a student might choose a shape from among a varied selection that will feature his name and be added to a special recognition display board that spotlights student accomplishments.

Putting It All Together Step by Step

Now that you have all the necessary components to start using Literacy Bin Activities in your classroom, how do you put it all together? What does a Literacy Bin Activities classroom look like? In the following section, we outline one approach to presenting and using Literacy Bin Activities and illustrate what it looks like in an actual classroom. Our sample is the fourth-grade classroom of Ms. Brighton (pseudonym). She has three homogeneous reading groups, each containing seven students. She is using three different books for instruction that she feels correspond adequately to the levels of her reading groups.

Step 1

Determine which of your instructional reading units you would like to supplement with a Literacy Bin and adopt the theme. If you feel your theme is too narrow or too large, either broaden or narrow it for use in the Literacy Bin.

In Ms. Brighton's classroom, she introduces her reading unit on tall tales to her students in a whole-class format by activating their prior knowledge about the genre, by introducing some vocabulary, and in accordance with other well-known prereading activities. She also introduces the comprehension strategies that she plans to cover during her small-group instruction.

Step 2

Determine whether you wish to use (or modify) a thematic game board that is already prepared and included in Appendix A. Until your material selection is complete (see step 3), you may be unsure of the kind of modifications that may be necessary. As you create your Literacy Bin and the activities contained therein, you may find the need to go back and forth between steps 2 and 3 as you discover materials to use and devise and revise your board activities accordingly.

In Ms. Brighton's classroom, she introduces the Tall Tale Literacy Bin by distributing a game board to each student and reviewing the activities. She may stand by the Literacy Bin and pull out materials, read sections of the instructions, or display books or other materials that may be needed to complete the activities as she explains.

Step 3

You will need to locate materials to use with your activities. Even if you decide to work with the prepared game boards that appear in Appendix A, it will still be necessary for you to locate reading passages, books, and other materials necessary for students to complete the activities. Keep in mind that you can start by using materials that you have on hand and supplement slowly. In our experience, we did not need to purchase many reading materials for our Literacy Bin Activities, and we did not purchase any art supplies. Still, we had amassed over time a very good, diverse collection of books that we used in our guided reading instruction and often pulled books out of this instructional collection for use in our Literacy Bins. Another way we began was by searching through our district's booklists and book rooms (our district's books were contained in two areas) and were pleasantly surprised to find collections and mixed sets of works that, although not having been used for instruction in years, were perfectly matched to or suitable for our Literacy Bin Activities. In addition to these suggestions, you may also wish to review the Resource Listings that appear at the ends of Chapters 3–6.

It is important to keep in mind that multiple copies of materials may be necessary to include in the Literacy Bin compartments. Students should have access to the materials they will need to complete each activity. Although our typical class size averages 20 students, the only activity for which we include 20 copies are some of the Vocabulary Knowledge and Word Skill activities because of their popularity. For all others, we included 5–10 copies and kept a master copy in a plastic envelope at the bottom of each compartment, so copies can be made as necessary. Creating a real-time procedure to get additional copies might be a consideration you will want to work out in advance. For example, we typically allow two students to go to the office (where our copies are made) to make five copies at a time, placing the extras in the Literacy Bin compartment with the master in its plastic envelope. Again, the teacher is not disturbed during this process and the students can independently solve the problem of running out of copies.

Additionally, we never found it necessary to include 20 copies of a single title in a compartment even if the book was used for a specific activity. Instead, we might include 5–8 copies and build into our procedures ways in which students can share materials. Teachers seem to possess an inherent skill for finding workable solutions in response to a lack of classroom materials; this skill will come in handy when assembling Literacy Bins.

Step 4

You will now need to consider preparing directions to accompany your Literacy Bin Activities. In your first Literacy Bin, you may wish to include directions that are very specific. Over time, the need for specificity may decline, especially as activities are repeated across themes. In your directions, you may want to include the titles of books or refer students to the Literacy

Bin Library that you have assembled, which contains an assortment of mixed thematic books. Sample activity directions appear in Appendix A and may serve as helpful guides. In preparing good directions, the single greatest criterion to keep in mind is that they should enable students to work independently; just the right blending of detail and simplicity seems best.

Step 5

Introduce your Literacy Bin and get your students started with their activities. In Ms. Brighton's classroom, she will meet with the first group of readers. She has assigned independent reading and a written response to her second group, and she instructs her third group to begin a Literacy Bin Activity.

After an interval of time (15–30 minutes), Ms. Brighton assigns independent work to her first group and dismisses them. They will read additional pages in their book and practice applying the comprehension strategies that were modeled and monitored through guided practice during instruction. They have been instructed to begin a Literacy Bin Activity when they complete this assignment. Ms. Brighton then meets with her second group, who have already read pages from their leveled book and prepared a written response. Ms. Brighton will begin her small-group instruction by having them take turns reading their response aloud. The third group may either continue working on the Literacy Bin Activities or stop working on them and begin reading from their leveled book in preparation for their small-group instruction.

After another interval (15–30 minutes), Ms. Brighton assigns independent work to her second group and dismisses them. They will read additional pages in their book and practice what they learned in their small-group instruction. Upon completion of this assigned work, they can then work on Literacy Bin Activities. Last, Ms. Brighton meets with the third group for instruction, and the first group will be involved in Literacy Bin Activities.

After a third interval (15–30 minutes), Ms. Brighton assigns independent work to her third group and dismisses them. She informs them that they will have time to complete their independent work at the start of reading time tomorrow, as she will not meet with them first. She then spends a brief amount of time (5–15 minutes) reviewing the students' work on the Literacy Bin Activities using a quick-check approach (see Chapter 7).

Students are then instructed to place all of their materials in their reading folder (including their leveled books, tic-tac-toe game board, and activities in progress) and prepare for whatever comes next in their schedule, instruction in another curriculum area such as math or social studies, a special activity such as an art class or the library, or lunch or recess.

Table 3 represents a visual overview of the movements and actions of this sample classroom. This model might be considered ideal in that the teacher is meeting with and providing instruction to three different reading groups every day (for 15 minutes or more).

In addition to having a great deal of flexibility in how you choose to use the Literacy Bins alongside your instruction, you are also allowed tremendous flexibility and support should you need to adjust your plans based on your students' immediate needs. For example, if one of your reading groups is struggling to identify the main idea in an informational reading passage that you have assigned, you may decide to work with them for a longer period of time, knowing that this quick change of plan will not result in leaving students within your other groups neglected, unchallenged, or involved in busy work.

Resource Materials

Finding materials for use in your Literacy Bins often seems like a big job. Although many teachers we work with soon recognize that they have access to good start-up resources, keep in mind that you do not need a class set of materials. You can make use of materials you already use, such as the daily newspaper or general news magazines. You also may have access to free or inexpensive materials through the Internet or by accessing educational or content-specific websites. Additionally, some of your Literacy Bin Activities may be based on ideas (and resources) you may already use in your classroom. As a final word of encouragement, the format of the Literacy Bin Activities, as well as the makeup of the entire Literacy Bin, is very flexible, and you can use and reuse materials creatively. Some examples to illustrate how to tap into these resources follow.

Often we have single or too few copies of trade books relating to our units of study. These could have been books purchased by a teacher through a book club or a parent–teacher organization, or a former student may have donated them to your school or even to your classroom library.

Table 3. Implementation Model for Small-Group Instruction and Use of Literacy Bin Activities

Time	Whole Class	Group 1	Group 2	Group 3
9:00–9:15	Introduction to tall tales			
9:15–9:25	Introduction to Literacy Bin Activities			
9:25–9:30	Instructions for small-group activities			
9:30–9:45		Teacher-led small-group instruction with students using leveled reader and Read-Along Guide	Students reading independently from leveled reader and writing a response in Read-Along Guide	Students selecting and working on Literacy Bin Activity
9:45–10:00		Independent follow-up activities with students reading from leveled reader and Read-Along Guide practice	Teacher-led small-group instruction with students using leveled reader and Read-Along Guide	Students continuing to work on Literacy Bin Activity or directed to independent reading from leveled reader and written response in Read-Along Guide
10:00–10:15		Students continue independent follow-up activities from leveled reader and Read-Along Guide; upon completion, may select and begin Literacy Bin Activity	Independent follow-up activities with students reading from leveled reader and Read-Along Guide practice (if desired); upon completion, may select and begin Literacy Bin Activity	Teacher-led small-group instruction with students using leveled reader and Read-Along Guide; assignment of independent follow-up (if desired)
10:15–10:30	Students continue work from above while teacher monitors student progress			

Note. Length of time meeting with each group may vary, based on needs identified by the teacher. Based on the time allotted for literacy activities, teachers may wish to meet with only two groups on the day the Literacy Bin Activities are introduced. Read-Along Guide activities can be replaced by other instructional activities.

There may not be enough for guided reading instruction, but these books can easily be put to good use in your Literacy Bins. Literacy Bin Activities that require reference or research will need materials, and providing a selection of texts at hand increases the students' ability to complete these tasks independently.

Many teachers we work with save newspaper and magazine articles related to areas of interest. These can be laminated, kept in a plastic sleeve, or kept in a folder to be used for a variety of Literacy Bin Activities. In addition to general newspapers and magazines, teacher resource magazines often have tear-out or reproducible games that may be used for Literacy Bins. Many of these games can be laminated or glued onto cardboard to make them more durable. Your school's library may periodically need to find a good home for older serial publications in order to make room for the new ones, and these could contain great ideas for Literacy Bin Activities. Likewise, you can repurpose old games for use in Literacy Bins; for example, an old jigsaw puzzle can be labeled with a question on the back of the puzzle piece and the answer on the tray or frame.

In addition to using game ideas from magazines, many activities can be created inexpensively using common supplies. For example, you can create scenario cards, puzzles, matching games, sequencing games, and many other activities using index cards, pictures cut from magazines, or old posters. Simply stapling small pages together can make a flipbook. While large sheets of construction paper can be teaching posters, old art materials or household scraps may be just the right item for a Literacy Bin Activity, too. Students can often help to create games to share with their classmates.

Many publishing companies now offer a wide range of text styles relating to all curriculum areas. Plays, Readers Theatre, graphic texts, dual-language texts, and multilevel texts are now easily available and of increasingly improving content. The Internet has many sites (some free and some through subscription) that have downloadable text, plays, and Readers Theatre in a huge range of levels and themes.

Clever ideas are free! Genius TV Talk Show is a clever drama activity that can be reused with different strategies and themes. It is free and requires few materials. Directions for this activity appear in Appendix A. (Although we typically provide a sample script or a few prompts to be used as a starting point, students may be able to do this alone if given adequate directions.) Creating television commercials and writing book reviews, poetry, and plays do not require many materials and are easily reused.

The ways to use the computer for Literacy Bins are vast and growing. There are many websites where students can practice their reading comprehension strategies or look for relevant information. They can create slideshows, music videos, and brochures, as well as write their own plays, stories, and poetry.

Looking for ideas in books and magazines and on the Internet is a surefire way to get started. Sharing ideas with colleagues will also make the job of getting started easier. Once you have a few Literacy Bins complete, the process gets easier!

You might also wish to encourage students to share their completed activities with others to spark ideas or to inspire. Viewing videotaped or live performances or participating in nature activities could be just the thing that captures the enthusiasm of others.

MOVING FORWARD

We encourage you to join the many teachers who have launched Literacy Bins in their classrooms, knowing that your move forward will result in success! The information provided in Chapters 3–6 will provide you with ideas in the form of sample game pieces that could work within the tic-tac-toe grids. As you read through these chapters, you might wish to flag those that align with the needs of your class, individual students, or with ideas of your own. You might also wish to jot down new ideas that come to you as you read the chapters. Let the games begin!

CHAPTER 3

Activities to Strengthen Comprehension Practice

B y the time they reach the intermediate grades, most students have mastered many decoding skills and are gaining fluency. However, do these students truly understand what they read? Comprehension of a text is absolutely essential if readers are to gain understanding of what they are reading. Recently, comprehension strategy instruction has taken a prominent role in literacy education, and strategy-based instruction has become a common fixture in elementary education.

In this chapter, you will learn about the foundational research supporting strategy-based comprehension instruction. You will also learn how the Literacy Bin Activities have been created to support and supplement strategy-based reading instruction, using our Quality Comprehension Model (Athans & Devine, 2008). A wealth of fun-tastic activities that you can use with your students for comprehension strategy practice also follow. Last, a listing of helpful resources on strategy-based comprehension and other related topics you might wish to use or consult concludes the chapter. It is important to note that the fun-tastic activities described in this chapter are flexible and can be used with many different reading approaches or reshaped to address particular strategies used within your district.

What Is Strategy-Based Comprehension?

Experts and researchers agree that there are skills and strategies that good readers use to gain meaning from text. Guided reading practices espoused by literacy authorities, such as Fountas and Pinnell (1996, 2001, 2006; Pinnell & Fountas, 2002), Harvey and Goudvis (2000), Keene and Zimmermann (2007), and Monroe (2002), concur that there are strategies and skills that can be taught to maximize one's reading comprehension.

In arriving at these understandings, researchers studied the behaviors of good readers and identified strategies these skilled readers used that enabled them to comprehend text. Although skilled readers were able to use their repertoire of strategies automatically, researchers believed that through the use of direct instruction, these same strategies could be taught to struggling readers. The number of strategies used by good readers and which among them is more critical than others remains a matter of pedagogical debate. As an example, reciprocal teaching (Palincsar & Brown, 1984) is a strategy-based instructional framework that focuses on four strategies: predicting, summarizing, asking questions, and clarifying. Meanwhile, the popular *7 Keys to Comprehension: How to Help Your Kids Read It and Get It!* by Zimmermann and Hutchins (2003) encourages the use of seven strategies: using background knowledge, creating mental images, questioning, inferring, determining importance, synthesizing, and monitoring for meaning. Despite these differences, literacy experts generally concur that strategy-based comprehension instruction works.

The Quality Comprehension Model

The literacy strategies included in this book are patterned after the ones we use in our Quality Comprehension Model (Athans & Devine, 2008). The strategies are not new or unique; rather, we have selected and refined those that align best with our students' needs and our curriculum. Table 4 lists the 17 comprehension strategies that we have identified as critical to intermediate students. We call the first eight strategies "the foundational eight." These are vital in helping students learn to read. The remaining strategies we refer to as the "skill-building nine." These are sometimes called outcome skills, because they are often demonstrated by proficient readers.

As described in the Preface, the focus of this model is to offer targeted reading comprehension instruction within small, homogeneous groups. Students use reading materials that are matched with their abilities, and the teacher provides direct instruction in the strategies listed in Table 4 (usually clustering two or three together within one reading unit). Group instruction typically follows the well-known gradual release of responsibility model espoused by Pearson and Gallagher (1983): instruction, modeling, guided practice, and independent work. Each student works within a

Table 4. The 17 Comprehension Strategies of the Quality Comprehension Model

Comprehension Strategies	Description
1. Using fix-up methods when meaning is challenged	1. When meaning is lost, students must become aware and take action by rereading a passage, reviewing earlier sections, or reading onward for about two sentences.
2. Finding word meaning and building vocabulary using context clues	2. Coming across new and unknown words is common. Sounding out, chunking, and linking words are tools to aid us while using context clues to make meaning of words or phrases.
3. Using visual text clues to figure out meaning	3. Text features, such as punctuation, font, spacing, titles, and subtitles, give clues to aid meaning.
4. Asking questions to engage in the text	4. Engaged readers ask and answer who, what, when, where, and how questions as they read.
5. Making connections to aid understanding	5. Prior knowledge and experience help us connect to our reading and in turn build our knowledge.
6. Visualizing to support the text	6. Readers make pictures in their minds of the people, places, or events they're reading about.
7. Making predictions	7. Engaged readers often make logical predictions about what will happen next in the story.
8. Synthesizing to gain new meaning	8. Students construct new meaning to build their knowledge and even create new understandings.
9. Finding the important or main idea	9. The important idea is the point or message conveyed in the passage.
10. Identifying facts and details	10. These facts and details provide substance to a reading passage and support important and main ideas.
11. Telling fact from opinion	11. Distinguishing fact from opinion helps readers build a deeper understanding of their reading.
12. Understanding sequence	12. Making sense of the order in which ideas are presented enables students to build comprehension.

(continued)

Table 4. The 17 Comprehension Strategies of the Quality Comprehension Model (*continued*)

Comprehension Strategies	Description
13. Comparing and contrasting	13. Considering ways in which ideas relate to something else, either through similarities or differences, is an avenue to develop understanding.
14. Interpreting figurative language	14. Understanding creative techniques authors use to convey meaning, such as similes, metaphors, and personification, helps aid comprehension.
15. Recognizing cause-and-effect relationships	15. Understanding relationships between ideas helps students grasp meaning by linking outcomes to causes.
16. Drawing conclusions and making inferences	16. Students often use a "sixth sense" or their inferential skills to interpret actions, events, or characters' motives or feelings.
17. Summarizing	17. Providing a brief description of critical information is one way students can hone their comprehension.

Read-Along Guide, an innovative written component that supports the comprehension strategy instruction during each phase of this instruction.

The use of Literacy Bin Activities supports and supplements our strategy-based guided reading instruction (and others like it) in two ways. First, the Literacy Bin Activities provide students with extra practice of the same two or three strategies that students are learning and practicing within their small-group instruction. The difference, however, is that the strategy practice activities in the Literacy Bin are multimodal, address varying learning styles, and adopt the "fun-tastic" charm that is characteristic of all Literacy Bin Activities. Second, the Literacy Bin Activities align with the theme-based reading unit. Rather than the students changing subject matter or theme as they make the transition from guided reading instruction to their work in the Literacy Bins, students have a variety of ways to practice and apply their skills while working within the current area of study. This often enables students to consider new ways of thinking about and building their knowledge of content information.

Why Is Strategy-Based Comprehension Instruction Important?

Strategy-based instruction provides teachers and students with a clear focus and the means to monitor different aspects of comprehension. Strategy-based instruction also provides a common, explicit language to use as a foundation for reading instruction. The clear direction and objectives, as well as the common language, help with the improvement and monitoring of critical reading skills. With such a clearly outlined structure, it is easier to pinpoint areas of strength and weakness, which then gives a more focused direction to planning and instruction.

Oftentimes, reading instruction revolves around preselected text. With strategy-based instruction, the focus is on the comprehension strategy and can be applied to any type of reading. Strategy-based instruction is flexible and tailored to meet the needs of various learners.

Literacy Bin Activities to Build Strategy-Based Instruction

The Literacy Bin Activities in this chapter are examples of ideas you could use to help students practice applying well-known reading comprehension strategies. Ideas for all 17 strategies we use are provided, yet you can determine which of them align with your instruction or with your district's approach to literacy improvement. Many of the activities might also help reinforce other objectives, such as constructing background knowledge or building vocabulary and word skills (as discussed in greater detail in Chapters 4 and 5), yet their focus here is to enable students to practice comprehension strategies.

For each of the 17 comprehension strategies, a brief description of an activity is presented in a game piece. You will also find alternative activity suggestions that can be used in place of the one provided or, should you wish to have students practice the same strategy within another Literacy Bin you use later in the school year, you can use these alternative suggestions to offer variety. For example, you might wish to repeat the use of the strategy summarizing. By using one of the alternative ideas, you are assured that the activity will attract students despite their having practiced that same strategy in a Literacy Bin used earlier in the year. Still, we have found that students enjoy having many of the activities repeated. The decision is up to you.

The Foundational Eight Strategies

Strategy 1: Using Fix-Up Methods When Meaning Is Challenged.
Students use this strategy when they realize they are having some difficulty with gaining meaning from the text. Although some students are skilled at monitoring their level of understanding, others may be unfamiliar with the notion that they need to take action if they are confused or if they have lost meaning. Some common "fix-up" actions include rereading the passage, revisiting other parts of the text, or reading on for about two sentences. Some fun-tastic activities to assist students in developing this awareness and in taking action include the following:

Figure 13. Literacy Bin Activity Game Board Square for Strategy 1

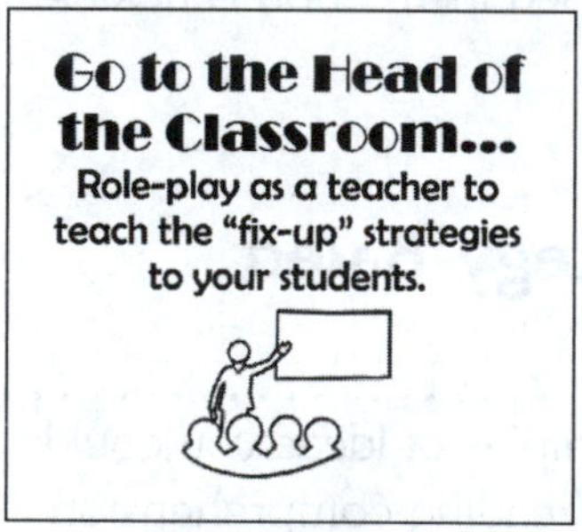

Go to the Head of the Classroom...
Role-play as a teacher to teach the "fix-up" strategies to your students.

- Role-playing "teacher" (see Figure 13)
- Renaming each fix-up action using symbols, acronyms, or wordplay
- Creating a song or rhyme to help remember each fix-up action

Strategy 2: Finding Word Meaning and Building Vocabulary Using Context Clues.
Finding word meaning through the use of context clues is a critical skill many teachers use within their strategy-based comprehension instruction. Students use this strategy when they come across unknown or unusual words. We include this strategy here should you wish to consider it among your comprehension strategies; however, we also devote Chapter 4 to many more activities that help students develop strong skills with words. Some common ways students can help learn word meaning and build their vocabulary include sounding out words, chunking words to look for

recognizable word parts, using context clues, and thinking about what makes sense. Activities to help students practice this skill include the following:

- Interpreting comic strips
- Interpreting quotes (see Figure 14)
- Writing a story using content vocabulary
- Playing homonym games

Figure 14. Literacy Bin Activity Game Board Square for Strategy 2

"May I Quote You?"

Read each of these famous quotes and rewrite them in your own words.

In addition to reviewing the activities listed here, you may also want to review the activities appearing in Chapter 4.

Strategy 3: Using Visual Text Clues to Figure Out Meaning. With this strategy, students use text features, such as punctuation, font, and subtitles, to aid meaning. Although some students recognize the importance of using these visual text clues to help them make meaning from text, others pay little attention to them and often struggle making sense of a passage. Therefore, helping students interpret and recognize the importance of these clues is the objective of this strategy. Additionally, young readers who are skilled with text features often found in fiction may not be as familiar with features found in nonfiction, such as reading text that appears in double columns on the page, so this strategy becomes especially helpful in introducing students to nonfiction texts. Activities to help students practice this strategy include the following:

Figure 15. Literacy Bin Activity Game Board Square for Strategy 3

OOOPS!!
Someone forgot to edit this story!
You must rewrite the story to correct spacing, punctuation, etc., so that it makes sense.

- Editing (see Figure 15)
- Creating text clue posters to decorate the classroom

Strategy 4: Asking Questions to Engage in Text. With this strategy, students ask and answer who, what, where, when, and why questions as they read. Passive readers are often unaware of their role in constructing

Figure 16. Literacy Bin Activity Game Board Square for Strategy 4

> # "JEOPARDY"
>
> Work with a group of 2–4 students to create a "Jeopardy" game for the class. Read several of the books or articles from the basket and create leveled questions. Be prepared to quiz your classmates.

meaning, so we work with students to help them grasp how questioning can be used to build their understanding. Additionally, proficient readers may grasp deeper level meaning by extending their skills with questioning. Fun-tastic activities, such as the following, can address the needs of both types of readers:

- Playing "Jeopardy" (see Figure 16)
- Writing interview questions for the Genius TV Talk Show (see Appendix A)
- Choosing a book, writing a mystery story, and presenting the mystery to the class to see if the other students can solve the mystery

Strategy 5: Making Connections to Aid Understanding. Prior knowledge and experience help students connect to text and improve understanding. Encouraging students to make connections to a character, event, or some part of a passage or book they are reading will also greatly increase their ability to retain and recall information. Scaffolding students' prior knowledge by demonstrating how connections can be made and then practicing the skill is what the following fun-tastic activities seek to accomplish:

Figure 17. Literacy Bin Activity Game Board Square for Strategy 5

> ### Connection Caboodle
>
> Play with a partner. Each partner draws one scenario card and has to share a connection.
>
> *Challenge:* Can you make all three types of connections with one card?

- Making text-to-text, text-to-self, and text-to-world connections
- Writing a diary entry
- Playing the Connection Caboodle card game, in which scenario cards state content-related events with which students try to make connections (see Figure 17)

Strategy 6: Visualizing. When proficient readers are comprehending text, they make pictures in their minds of the people, places, or events they are reading about. Some students are unfamiliar with this strategy or struggle with learning how to visualize. There are many types of activities that can be used in the Literacy Bins to help ignite students' ability to conjure up mental pictures, so they might grasp meaning more readily. Helping students engage in and practice the strategy across literary genres and with works of fiction and nonfiction is another challenge the fun-tastic activities can help develop, such as the following:

- Creating a flipbook, also known as a zoetrope (see Figure 18)
- Making a mural
- Acting out a scene
- Creating a commercial

Figure 18. Literacy Bin Activity Game Board Square for Strategy 6

Zoetrope

(a device that creates an illusion of movement from a rapid succession of static, flipped pictures, also known as a flipbook)

Create a zoetrope about (current topic) for our class to enjoy.

Strategy 7: Making Predictions. With this strategy, students practice making logical predictions about what will happen next in a story. Some students may be skilled with this strategy, whereas others may be unable to base their prediction on logical events from the passage. Therefore, one goal of the following activities is to steer students toward more practical and appropriate predictions, while another goal is helping others extend their proficient skills:

- Pretending to travel in time using a "transporter machine" and describing what is happening in the future
- Pretending to be a fortune teller by devising a prediction and writing it on a paper crystal ball (see Figure 19)
- Creating story starters
- Writing a literary prediction like a weather forecaster predicting the weather

Figure 19. Literacy Bin Activity Game Board Square for Strategy 7

Fortune Teller

Use your fortune-telling skills to make a prediction about (current topic) and write about it on your crystal ball.

Strategy 8: Synthesize to Gain New Meaning. In this strategy, students are encouraged to build their knowledge, shape and reshape their understandings, and arrive at new meaning. Struggling readers may need help grasping this strategy, as it is often what interferes with their ability to comprehend a reading passage. Demonstrating how knowledge is built (often by using some of the other strategies) and then using the knowledge to arrive at new understandings are the objectives of the following fun-tastic activities:

Figure 20. Literacy Bin Activity Game Board Square for Strategy 8

PUZZLED

WHAT'S THE BIG PICTURE?

Create several puzzle pieces that go together to make a picture or shape related to (current theme). Each piece must contain relevant information or illustrations about (current theme).

- Writing "rounds" or canon stories (A group of students start with a themed or time period prompt, then working around the group, each student adds to the story.)
- Creating a slideshow presentation to share information on a topic
- Creating a puzzle illustrating how information is related using patterns to create puzzle pieces on stiff paper (see Figure 20)

The Skill-Building Nine Strategies

Strategy 9: Finding the Important or Main Idea. Students apply this strategy each time they read to determine the point or important idea in a passage. Often students are unable to prioritize main ideas from subordinating ones and are thus unable to glean critical information from a reading passage. The following activities encourage students to think critically about what is most important and provide them with practice in considering the significance of information:

Figure 21. Literacy Bin Activity Game Board Square for Strategy 9

What Was the Author Thinking?

Read one of the passages or short stories from the basket and fill in a "thought bubble" explaining the author's purpose.

- Participating in "What Was the Author Thinking?" (see Figure 21)
- Using different color highlighters to color-code important information from the reading passage
- Creating a slideshow highlighting the main idea
- Writing 10 important words or phrases on index cards that will help your classmates better understand the reading

Strategy 10: Identifying Facts and Details. With this strategy, students identify facts and details to support important and main ideas. Students are often asked to support their ideas or statements with details, yet this is a skill that requires some foundation. Therefore, helping students first identify facts and details and then showing them how to use them as support are the objectives of the following funtastic activities:

Figure 22. Literacy Bin Activity Game Board Square for Strategy 10

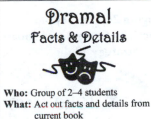

Drama!

Facts & Details

Who: Group of 2–4 students
What: Act out facts and details from current book
Where: Room 119

- A group of students acting out facts and details from the current text in a charades-style format (see Figure 22)

- Creating fact-based trading cards

- Identifying a set number of facts and details from the current text and creating a musical interpretation to share with the class

Strategy 11: Telling Fact From Opinion. With this strategy, students distinguish fact from opinion to help build a deeper understanding of the text. Critical readers are often able to distinguish statements of fact from statements of opinion. Still, helping students strengthen this skill, especially within the content areas, can be tricky. This is especially true if students have little background knowledge on a topic. The following activities can help all readers gain a greater degree of proficiency with this skill:

- Using information from a reading passage to create statements of facts and opinions and quizzing classmates (see Figure 23)

Figure 23. Literacy Bin Activity Game Board Square for Strategy 11

- Sorting excerpt cards into two piles: facts and opinions

Is That a Fact?

Use information from the reading passages to create fact and/or opinion statements. Quiz your classmates to see if they can tell which are which.

- Highlighting facts in one color and opinions in another color in a reading selection

- Using a different musical sound effect to differentiate facts and opinions while reading a passage out loud to the class

Strategy 12: Understanding Sequence. Students make sense of the order in which ideas are presented to enhance comprehension. Gaining proficiency with this strategy is especially helpful within the content areas of science and social studies, in which the ordering of events is critical. Additionally, as students are exposed to more complex fictional works, such as those that may use flashbacks, identifying time sequence to gain meaning is necessary. The following activities help strengthen student skill with this strategy:

Figure 24. Literacy Bin Activity Game Board Square for Strategy 12

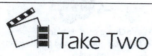 Take Two

Use a story from the basket or write one of your own. Act out the story for the class *twice:* first in the wrong sequence, then in the correct sequence.

- Acting out a story in correct and incorrect sequences to demonstrate how sequence affects meaning (see Figure 24)
- Mixing up the sequence of a story and having students rearrange the events, so they are in the correct order

Strategy 13: Compare and Contrast. With this strategy, students consider ways in which ideas relate to something else as a way to develop deeper understanding. In some reading passages, authors may even present information or ideas through relationships to other concepts and highlight ways in which they are similar or different. Therefore, the following activities help students recognize these relationships, and these activities also strengthen student ability to create similarities and differences between ideas independently:

Figure 25. Literacy Bin Activity Game Board Square for Strategy 13

Iroquois vs. Democracies

There are many similarities and differences between the early Iroquois and current democratic forms of governments. Create a Venn diagram poster to illustrate and teach your classmates about these similarities and differences.

- Creating a Venn diagram poster to show similarities and differences between two (or more) topics (see Figure 25)
- Holding a class debate about a current or content-related event
- Writing a compare-and-contrast essay to display or submit to a magazine or newspaper for children

Strategy 14: Interpreting Figurative Language. Students focus on working with similes, metaphors, personification, and other types of figurative language to help aid comprehension. Students often have trouble understanding meaning when authors express ideas using these figurative literary techniques. However, recognizing the more common techniques and developing an ability to interpret their meaning in a variety of literary settings is a skill students will need to grasp. The following fun-tastic activities are designed to help students with these objectives:

- Reading a variety of poems and label examples of figurative language and creating a minibook of the examples (see Figure 26)

- Choral reading famous quotes, story excerpts, or poems that have examples of figurative language

- Creating a figurative language bulletin board

Figure 26. Literacy Bin Activity Game Board Square for Strategy 14

You Crack Me Up!

Read through a selection of short stories and poems to record as many idioms as you can find. Create a book illustrating the literal and actual meanings of each phrase.

Strategy 15: Recognizing Cause-and-Effect Relationships. With this strategy, students learn about the relationships between ideas to help link outcomes to causes. Gaining a firm understanding of not only what is happening in a passage but also why it is happening provides students with a greater depth of understanding. The following fun-tastic activities encourage students to practice this skill:

- Matching cause and effect (see Figure 27)

- Having one student write a beginning event and the others in the group write a possible effect, then reading out loud to the class

- Using pictures cut from magazines as story starters, writing a story about what is happening in the pictures and the outcome

- Creating "Why Did That Happen?" flags that students can give to someone in their group while reading, then stopping to explain the cause-and-effect relationship

Figure 27. Literacy Bin Activity Game Board Square for Strategy 15

Cause-and-Effect Matching Game

Choose a "cause" from the pile and match it with a card from the "effect" pile. Discuss your match with a partner to see if you both agree.

Strategy 16: Drawing Conclusions and Making Inferences. Students practice using their "sixth sense," or inferencing skills, to interpret actions,

events, or characters' motives or feelings. As active readers become engaged in their reading, they rely on this sense to help them make meaning of the plot, explain events or actions, and piece together ideas without having to be explicitly told. The following Literacy Bin Activities can help students develop and refine this skill:

Figure 28. Literacy Bin Activity Game Board Square for Strategy 16

Get a Clue!

Use your inferencing skills to help solve the mystery! Read one event clue at a time and try to solve the mystery. Write down your solution, then read the answer in the "Mystery Solved" envelope.

- Playing the "Get a Clue!" game (see Figure 28)
- Playing the 20 questions game
- Writing a character biography
- Reading a story starter and writing and illustrating a conclusion

Strategy 17: Summarizing. With this strategy, students provide a brief description of critical information to hone their comprehension. Writing a concise summary can be difficult, and students benefit from continual practice in this skill. Evaluating ideas, then selecting which among them should be included, omitted, or combined with others, is tricky. The following fun-tastic activities help students develop these critical skills:

Figure 29. Literacy Bin Activity Game Board Square for Strategy 17

T.V. Commercial

Create a 60-second commercial

Convince others to read the book you have just finished reading. (When you are ready, sign up to be recorded on video.)

- Creating a television commercial (see Figure 29)
- Rewriting a story in cartoon format using speech bubbles
- Writing and performing a song that summarizes the reading
- Creating a slideshow presentation that summarizes the story

Comprehension Practice Resource Materials

State and National Standards

In addition to reviewing the activities presented in this chapter, we also encourage you to review your state or national standards to help you reshape these or devise new comprehension strategy activities. Guidelines provided for the standards may include key indicators that can provide reassurance that your activities align with the literacy standards. You might also find that your state education department may suggest other standards-based ideas that will be helpful.

State Assessments

You might also wish to review your state assessments to determine if test questions may be patterned after some of the comprehension strategies. For example, are students asked to predict what might happen next in a reading passage? Are students asked to determine the correct sequence of activities in a reading passage? Is the terminology used in your state tests similar to the terminology used in your strategy practice activities? Reviewing your state assessments could provide you with additional guidelines to follow as you devise these types of activities for use in your Literacy Bin.

Books

The following books are good resources that can provide you with more information about strategy-based reading comprehension. Many have been written by the literacy experts cited in this chapter. If your district's professional development library does not have these books, you could borrow them though an interlibrary loan system, which is often available through school districts or your local library.

- Athans, S.K., & Devine, D.A. (2008). *Quality Comprehension: A Strategic Model of Reading Instruction Using Read-Along Guides, Grades 3–6.* Newark, DE: International Reading Association.
- Curriculum Associates. (2000). *Strategies to Achieve Reading Success: STARS.* North Billerica, MA: Author.
- Fountas, I.C., & Pinnell, G.S. (1996). *Guided Reading: Good First Teaching for All Children.* Portsmouth, NH: Heinemann.
- Fountas, I.C., & Pinnell, G.S. (2001). *Guiding Readers and Writers, Grades 3–6: Teaching Comprehension, Genre, and Content Literacy.* Portsmouth, NH: Heinemann.

- Fountas, I.C., & Pinnell, G.S. (2006). *Teaching for Comprehending and Fluency: Thinking, Talking, and Writing About Reading, K–8*. Portsmouth, NH: Heinemann.

- Harvey, S., & Goudvis, A. (2000). *Strategies That Work: Teaching Comprehension to Enhance Understanding*. Portland, ME: Stenhouse.

- Harvey, S., & Goudvis, A. (2007). *Strategies That Work: Teaching Comprehension to Enhance Understanding* (2nd ed.). Portland, ME: Stenhouse.

- Keene, E.O., & Zimmermann, S. (2007). *Mosaic of Thought: The Power of Comprehension Strategy Instruction* (2nd ed.). Portsmouth, NH: Heinemann.

- McLaughlin, M., & Allen, M.B. (2002). *Guided Comprehension: A Teaching Model for Grades 3–8*. Newark, DE: International Reading Association.

- McLaughlin, M., & Allen, M.B. (2002). *Guided Comprehension in Action: Lessons for Grades 3–8*. Newark, DE: International Reading Association.

- Oczkus, L.D. (2003). *Reciprocal Teaching at Work: Strategies for Improving Reading Comprehension*. Newark, DE: International Reading Association.

- Strickland, D.S., Ganske, K., & Monroe, J.K. (2002). *Supporting Struggling Readers and Writers: Strategies for Classroom Intervention 3–6*. Portland, ME: Stenhouse; Newark, DE: International Reading Association.

Articles

If you or your district belongs to professional organizations, you may wish to search their periodicals for current information on strategy-based comprehension instruction and related topics. In many cases, articles can be downloaded free of charge or for a small fee.

Online Resources

Using search engines and keywords, such as *comprehension instruction*, *comprehension strategies*, and *reading instruction*, will help narrow your search for further information that may be helpful.

MOVING FORWARD

Remember, it is important to try to add variety and novelty to the way in which you provide instruction and practice using the comprehension strategies. Even if you use the same general ideas, create a game format in which to practice, as demonstrated in the models in this chapter. When students have trouble grasping and applying the comprehension strategies during your instruction, relying on these activities will enable you to give them additional practice.

CHAPTER 4

Activities to Build
Vocabulary and Word Skills

Today, we face some significant challenges in terms of helping our students build a strong and reliable vocabulary. Research confirms what many of us know or suspect from our daily classroom struggles: Students who reach fourth grade with limited vocabularies are very likely to struggle to understand grade-level texts (e.g., Chall & Jacobs, 2003; National Institute of Child Health and Human Development [NICHD], 2000; RAND Reading Study Group, 2002). If we rely on an instructional approach where we deliver a 10- to 20-word weekly vocabulary list, we will fall gravely short of equipping students with adequate word knowledge despite our best intentions. According to one estimate, the average U.S. student encounters nearly 10,000 unfamiliar words over the course of the fourth-grade year alone (Nagy & Anderson, 1984). Further, if we rely on *incidental* word learning, which is the word-building influence that naturally affects students from oral language and reading experiences taking place within classrooms, we may not be supporting our students' vocabulary growth efficiently. Explicit instruction and repeated exposure to extensive and vocabulary-rich reading materials may be better options (Yopp & Yopp, 2007).

As our curricula promise to grow even more rigorous, most literacy leaders agree that our vocabulary-building challenges must be met with a multifaceted and systematic approach to vocabulary instruction (e.g., Beck, McKeown, & Kucan, 2002; Flynt & Brozo, 2008; Graves, 2006; Kamil & Hiebert, 2005; Stahl & Nagy, 2006). The use of Literacy Bin Activities helps support such an approach.

In this chapter, you will find an overview of the critical understandings that literacy experts have uncovered in their research on vocabulary and word development. You will also learn how the Literacy Bin Activities that focus on word skills can easily support the larger framework of your literacy instruction. Last, an extensive assortment of fun-tastic activities for developing a content-rich vocabulary for every student is provided.

What Is Vocabulary Instruction?

According to literacy expert Beck, "vocabulary means learning *meanings* of new words" and it can also mean "words that a reader recognizes in print" (Beck, McKeown, & Kucan, 2008, p. 1). Although these meanings are easy to grasp, delving into them a little deeper exposes some complexities. There may be gradations of word knowledge that range from no knowledge to "rich decontextualized knowledge of a word" (p. 792), and to what degree does word recognition extend to variations of a word or word parts? To help address these important issues, literacy experts generally agree that a systematic and multifaceted approach to vocabulary and word-building skill instruction is necessary. Specific components include (a) providing students with direct instruction of keywords and word-learning strategies, (b) exposing students to extensive and vocabulary-rich reading, and (c) creating an environment that encourages students to develop a "word consciousness," described as interest in and curiosity about words (Graves, 2006; Yopp & Yopp, 2007).

Why Is Building Vocabulary and Word Skills Important?

The single greatest reason that vocabulary and word-skill development is important is because of its significant impact on comprehension. This is true in terms of general vocabulary development as well as for the development of *content* or *academic* vocabulary, which is word knowledge used with texts that are valued in school (Brozo & Simpson, 2007) or the words "necessary to learn and talk about academic subjects" (Kieffer & Lesaux, 2007, p. 135).

Studies supporting the strong relationship between vocabulary and comprehension are extensive and date back to the mid-1940s. Subsequent studies (Snow, Tabors, Nicholson, & Kurland, 1995) confirm similar findings for very young children and go so far as to suggest that kindergarten students' vocabulary knowledge is also a powerful predictor of students' reading comprehension in later years. Some experts claim the relationship holds as much as four years later (Wagner et al., 1997), whereas others believe it may extend to high school years (Cunningham & Stanovich, 1997). The strong relationship between vocabulary knowledge and reading comprehension is reaffirmed by the RAND Reading Study Group (2002) and leads other researchers to emphasize this significance for content texts that expose students to new and specialized words (Harmon, Hedrick, & Wood, 2005). In sum, students need general and specialized word knowledge to support their comprehension, and ongoing instruction is necessary.

In our experience, especially in the content areas, vocabulary and word skill is so critical for students in grades 2–6 that we felt it necessary to devote an entire chapter to ways in which Literacy Bin Activities can help target and strengthen student word abilities. Careful reflection of our classroom practices and those of other teachers with whom we've worked confirms that additional word activities need to be in place to provide the multifaceted approach literacy experts recommend. As an example, within our guided reading lessons through use of a Read-Along Guide (described in the Preface), we integrate content-based vocabulary and word-skill instruction. Specifically, we teach, practice, and monitor students' use of word-attack strategies that use context and morphology clues (i.e., breaking words apart). Dictionary and glossary skills are also covered. Here, students record new words they encounter and apply word-attack strategies to construct meaning. Entries are discussed during guided reading instruction with teacher support and guidance. Teachers may choose vocabulary words for students, students may self-select words, or there may be a combination of both approaches. We also teach specialized vocabulary words that students encounter across the curriculum. These words appear in our content texts or reading materials and reflect the suggestions of our content teachers or other specialists. Finally, we provide spelling and general word-building instruction using a popular packaged program. Like many school districts, we incorporate this instruction outside of the time allotted for reading.

Our Literacy Bin Activities are designed to support and extend all of these efforts: (a) reinforce key content words, (b) encourage word-attack and word-building skill practice, (c) increase exposure to vocabulary-rich activities, and (d) help build word consciousness in unique ways. In keeping with the recommendation of literacy experts, you might wish to review your collective vocabulary and word-building activities and, after reviewing information presented in this chapter, consider how the use of Literacy Bin Activities will best supplement them.

From our own research with these activities, we identified several patterns:

1. All students benefit from vocabulary and word-skill development. Interestingly, our struggling and proficient readers initially demonstrated a greater willingness to apply word-attack skills in comparison with their highly proficient classmates who seemed unaccustomed to the skill.

2. Ongoing instruction and practice is necessary, and we continued with all avenues of instruction and practice throughout the school year.

3. Students who demonstrated strong word and vocabulary skill can successfully manipulate numerous approaches together to infer and confirm new word meaning.

Many literacy experts support a game approach to help students develop word and vocabulary skills and word consciousness as the result of the research-based benefits of word games (e.g., Blachowicz & Fisher, 2004; Padak & Rasinski, 2005). Providing students with explicit and systematic instruction as well as "playful and interactive follow-up" (Beck et al., 2002, p. 1) is an approach that many of us already use within our classrooms.

Many of the activities in this chapter refer to a vocabulary list or rely on the use of reading passages that include vocabulary words. These words are selected by you and align with the theme of the Literacy Bin. After you've decided on your word selection, determine which games might work best with it. For example, your word list for a unit on government might be rich with words derived from Latin and Greek, so selecting root word–analysis activities could be good for this unit. You might also wish to keep in mind skills and strategies you have already taught that can easily be incorporated into your Literacy Bin Activities. For example, if you've provided instruction on word-attack skills, asking students to use these strategies independently or with minor monitoring within the activities should not be an unrealistic expectation.

Keeping the atmosphere light and enjoyable is the best way to encourage students to engage in wordplay games. Also, ensuring that students don't become frustrated while interacting in these activities is key. Determining the best way to coordinate your explicit instruction with the games will be critical and may require careful monitoring at first (see Chapter 7). Still, the benefits of the game activities will quickly become evident.

Literacy Bin Activities to Build Vocabulary and Word Skills

The Literacy Bin Activities presented in this chapter are examples of ideas you could use to build vocabulary and word skills. Many activities may also help reinforce other objectives, such as constructing background knowledge or developing fluency (and may appear in those chapters, too), yet their emphasis here is on working with words, their meanings, and their structure. A general description of each activity and suggestions for ways in which it could be modified are provided. Information you might wish to place in the Literacy Bin compartment, such as instructions or student materials, are also listed (see Appendix A for examples). Use the activities featured here, modify them as you wish, or create your own using these as models. As you review the activities, you might also consider materials you have available or can readily locate to use with an activity.

Imaginative Phonics

Students take a word list from the Literacy Bin and read each word very slowly, pronouncing each sound (see Figure 30). This comical activity encourages students to apply their skills with letter–sound relationships to unfamiliar content words. Including the names of significant individuals related to your theme, such as explorer Giovanni da Verrazano, and places of historic significance, such as the Caribbean, will help students tackle these tricky stumbling blocks. Students can perform in front of an audience, invite classmates to recite words with them, use technology to record their presentation, or even dress in character.

Figure 30. Literacy Bin Activity Game Board Square for Imaginative Phonics

Meet "S-t-r-e-t-c-h"

Stretch likes to s-t-r-e-t-c-h every sound in every word! Pretend you're Stretch and practice reading the vocabulary words by stretching out each sound. Deliver your stretched-out performance to classmates.

Figure 31. Literacy Bin Activity Game Board Square for Syllabification Snap-Alongs

Clap, Tap, and Snap!

Using the vocabulary list from the Literacy Bin, clap, tap, or snap the syllables for each of the words. Or create an imaginative, zany instrument to play during your performance and sing.

Figure 32. Literacy Bin Activity Game Board Square for Imaginative Characters

The Pronunci-ator!

You will compete in a contest to become the Pronuncia-tor—the voice of a world-renowned, online audio dictionary. Practice your words carefully and get ready to compete!

Figure 33. Literacy Bin Activity Game Board Square for Imaginative Word Games

UNDERCOVER!

Many words in your vocabulary list have smaller words hidden in them. See if you can spy all of the hidden words (and identify their meaning).

Super Spy Challenge:
How many new words can you make using letters from a vocabulary word?

Syllabification Snap–Alongs

Students use a word list from the Literacy Bin and create a rhythmic performance by breaking words into syllables (see Figure 31). Encouraging students to break apart multisyllabic words will help them with many other commonly used word-attack skills. Students can create an instrument or use one they already have. They can also group words with similar syllable patterns or be whimsical. You might wish to display each student's word list during the performances.

Imaginative Characters

Assuming the role of a comical character, the "Pronunci-ator," students practice pronouncing words from a vocabulary list in the Literacy Bin (see Figure 32). This activity helps students master difficult, multisyllabic words. Also, including words that stray from the standard rules of pronunciation may be a good way to clarify some of these troublesome words and challenge students as well (i.e., a Literacy Bin featuring the science theme electricity could include the word *solder*, pronounced "sod-der"). Students may want to work with others and stage a comical competition. Students can listen to words using an online audio dictionary.

Imaginative Word Games

Students use a vocabulary list from the Literacy Bin and locate root words and prefixes (see Figure 33). This activity is good if you've provided instruction in Greek and Latin roots, and your keyword list includes appropriate words. Other word-attack skills, such as those that uncover word derivatives, are also good choices for this activity (e.g., *government*, *govern, governor*). You might have students use letters in a word to make new words as an alternative or a challenge.

Spelling and Word Close-Ups

Students use a vocabulary list and rewrite words in a fancy style. Encourage students to carefully craft every letter for those troublesome and tricky words (see Figure 34). This activity helps build students' spelling skills within a content area and strengthens their word consciousness, too. You might want students to select five tricky words from the list and feature them in one picture. Using computers and any word program that has fun fonts is another way to engage students. Another variation of this game is to have students create a flag or poster for the time period or theme featured in the Literacy Bin (e.g., prehistoric times, dinosaurs) and decorate the flag with appropriate vocabulary words.

Figure 34. Literacy Bin Activity Game Board Square for Spelling and Word Close-Ups

Word Gallery Showcase
featuring
Visually Appealing Vocabulary

Craft your vocabulary words in a fancy, colorful, expressive way! Don't misspell any words and carefully construct every letter, so they're all "picture perfect." Share your favorites in the showcase!

Drawing Activities

Students create pictures of the words on their vocabulary list (see Figure 35). Encouraging students to attach a visual image to the new or unfamiliar word may help some students create a memorable connection to the word. This strategy works well in the early elementary grade levels as well as at the upper elementary levels. You might wish to have students create digital books and incorporate photographs or other visual technology.

Figure 35. Literacy Bin Activity Game Board Square for Drawing Activities

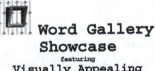

Picture This!

Make an illustrated picture book of the words on the vocabulary list. Be creative, have fun, and plan to share with a friend!

Drama Activities

In "Casting Call!" students act out words from a keyword list (see Figure 36). Suggesting that students use simple props may help them with words that are difficult to demonstrate through actions. Recalling the comical ways

Figure 36. Literacy Bin Activity Game Board Square for Drama Activities

Casting Call!

A fabulously famous Broadway producer has announced a casting call for a new production called "Wonderful Words of (Literacy Bin theme)." Find a buddy or two and practice rehearsing ways to portray the vocabulary words for this unit. Props and other imaginative devices are welcome!

Figure 37. Literacy Bin Activity Game Board Square for Using Online Websites

Virtual Scavenger Hunt

Select a website from those provided and hunt for nouns, verbs, adjectives, and adverbs that are variations of words from our vocabulary list.

Figure 38. Literacy Bin Activity Game Board Square for Trading Cards

Trading Cards

Design and create a set of colorful, information-packed trading cards for all of this unit's vocabulary words. In addition to including the definition, add other very cool tidbits about each word. Swap with a friend.

in which students may perform content words often enables others to remember the meaning of the word. Students may wish to work alone or in small groups. Suggesting that students consider three different ways to convey a word meaning may encourage a deeper level of understanding.

Use of Online Websites

Students are provided with websites to visit and are asked to locate specific words or other targeted categories of words related to the thematic Literacy Bin (see Figure 37). This activity helps students develop their online reading skills while also strengthening their content vocabulary. Many educational sites also include links that may help students with difficult content words (i.e., many sites highlight words that link to definitions provided in a dictionary or other resource). You might wish to include some type of web or chart for students to use as they search online.

Trading Cards

Students work with a vocabulary list and create imaginative trading cards (see Figure 38). You might wish to suggest specific information for students to include on the cards. For example, students might be asked to include a picture or diagram with labels on the face of the card and then provide a sentence that uses the word correctly in context on the back. Using visuals and demonstrating proper usage in a sentence reinforces a students' understanding of hard-to-master vocabulary words. This activity can also be modified to make use of computer software such as PowerPoint.

Creative Competitions

Students work with their word list and available resources to locate information about their words (see Figure 39). As shown on the game piece, suggesting that students locate word origins, word variations, and other activities that require research will help build their in-depth word knowledge. The categories you select may depend on your vocabulary list. You might wish to provide a web or other organizer to help students record and plan their research. This is a great follow-up activity once students are familiar with using classroom resources.

Figure 39. Literacy Bin Activity Game Board Square for Creative Competitions

Who Has the Deepest Understanding?

Find two or three friends to stage a friendly word competition. Explore your keywords using classroom resources to identify meaning, variations, synonyms, antonyms, word origin, and other exciting information. Share your deep understanding as contestants in this hilarious new game show!

The New Game Show!

Unique Sorting Activity

The word sorting activity featured here can easily be used for a variety of Literacy Bin themes to help students reflect on the relationship among words on their list. Thinking critically about these relationships supports a more in-depth knowledge of students' content-based word lists. Students use a vocabulary list or cards from the Literacy Bin and group and record their words into numerous categories (see Figure 40). You might wish to supply an organizer for students to explain and record their word groupings.

Figure 40. Literacy Bin Activity Game Board Square for Unique Sorting Activities

Sort of Lost & Out of Sorts

Your vocabulary words are lost and alone. Help them hook up with other words. Group them together in categories you create. See how many different ways you can help your words find new friends.

Unique Word Jumbles

Students use a sheet provided in the Literacy Bin that has letters that are jumbled or broken into morphemes and scattered throughout (see Figure 41). Activities like this cause students to take a closer look at words and manipulate sounds and letters in ways that build and support word knowledge.

Figure 41. Literacy Bin Activity Game Board Square for Unique Word Jumbles

Cafeteria Calamity

Yikes! Your vocabulary words got into a food fight in the cafeteria! Pieces of words are *everywhere!* It's up to you to tidy up and put them back together!

Food Fight!

If a "Cafeteria Calamity" does not correspond well to the theme of your Literacy Bin, there are numerous others that could work (e.g., a fairy tales–themed Literacy Bin could feature beanstalk leaves with morphemes). You might wish to create a word sheet containing jumbled words using the Internet or easy-to-use tools available in your word-processing software. Simple word jumbles or word search games can be used here as well.

Word–Learning Demonstrations

Using context clues within content-area or informational reading is often tricky for some students. Helping them creatively figure out ways to learn the meaning of new words through this strategy can be a very powerful new tool for many. In "Word Learners Are Awesome!" students use a passage from the Literacy Bin to demonstrate their use of context clues to figure out meaning (see Figure 42). Listening to others talk and reason their way through this process is often eye-opening to some students. Students might wish to dress in character and use props, such as posters that explain common context-clue strategies.

Figure 42. Literacy Bin Activity Game Board Square for Word-Learning Demonstrations

Word Learners Are Awesome!

Everybody wants to be a totally cool, totally effective word learner! Yeah!

Here's your totally cool chance to teach the class everything you know about using context clues to figure out new words. Use a passage from the Literacy Bin to show them how it's done.

Creative Poetry

Students use the vocabulary list to create a poem for display (see Figure 43). You might wish to include a review sheet of the various types of poetry you have studied or provide several examples for students to follow. For example, students might wish to make shape poems, in which vocabulary words are constructed into an appropriate shape. Another hit with students are acrostic poems. Many creative forms of poetry would work well with this activity. Spelling skills as well as word awareness can be strengthened through this activity.

Figure 43. Literacy Bin Activity Game Board Square for Creative Poetry

Poetry Vocabulary

Use your vocabulary list to create some creative poetry. Use your imagination and your great sense of word savvy to create a literary masterpiece!

Comical Characters for Word-Attack Skills

Students use a passage from the Literacy Bin in which vocabulary words have been replaced by nonsensical words and use context clues to figure out which real words belongs in their place (see Figure 44). Using the "Professor" as a comical character to launch the activity is a lighthearted way to invite students to try out this skill, which is often perceived as being very difficult. You might also challenge students to use the context in a variety of ways, such as through using clues that provide a definition, including an antonym, or relying on a synonym. In addition to using thematic vocabulary words, you might also wish to use spelling or general vocabulary words. Provide students with a master word list.

Figure 44. Literacy Bin Activity Game Board Square for Comical Characters for Word-Attack Skills

Professor Gobble-de-Gook

The professor is rather strange and replaces new vocabulary words with gobble-de-gook to try to stump students. See if you can identify the correct word that actually belongs in the passage from the master word list. Don't forget to use your ptbpwqt (context) clues.

Creative Connections

Students use a passage from the Literacy Bin in which vocabulary words or key phrases have been highlighted. They use a think-aloud technique to describe ways they connect to a word (see Figure 45). For example, as students encounters the phrase *renewable resources* in an informational passage from a Literacy Bin on geography, they may recall a family trip to a state park where replanting efforts were underway and comment on their understanding that trees are renewable resources. Using prompts such as "This reminds me of ..." is one way to invite students to make connections to new vocabulary words. This activity works well with hard-to-read documents, such as the Constitution, as students provide their kid-friendly interpretation of keywords, phrases, and ideas using personal connections.

Figure 45. Literacy Bin Activity Game Board Square for Creative Connections

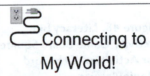

Connecting to My World!

Can you connect to these highlighted vocabulary words? Read a passage aloud and perform a think-aloud, giving us your take on the vocabulary words. Plug in your brains, have fun, and show us how you're connected!

Advice Activities

Students perform a radio talk show to share their general views about words and their thoughts on the vocabulary words. By having students play

Figure 46. Literacy Bin Activity Game Board Square for Advice Activities

Talking About Words on the Air

Assume the role of a radio talk show personality and share your ideas about words. Discuss what you like about them, how they make you feel, ways you interact with them, and more. Be sure to include some specifics about the vocabulary words in this unit.

Figure 47. Literacy Bin Activity Game Board Square for Using Book-Format and Other Graphic Organizers

Closest Thing to a Paper Airplane!

Fasten your seatbelts and take off!
Record fun-filled vocabulary facts in
a foldable graphic organizer.
Engage in this fantastic journey.

Figure 48. Literacy Bin Activity Game Board Square for Activities With Word Manipulatives

Construction Site Word Building

Using the materials provided, create your vocabulary word. Share your word-construction activities with a friend and be prepared to discuss interesting observations about your words.
(building materials included)

off of the popular advice shows format, they may think more deeply about words and come to realize a new appreciation for word sounds and structures. As an example, the multisyllabic *onomatopoeia*, used in a poetry-based Literacy Bin to describe the creative technique where a word imitates a sound, is a kid-friendly favorite that generates a lot of discussion. You may wish to simulate a radio show using GarageBand, which is easy-to-use recording software, or other audiovisual technology (see Figure 46). Students may also wish to perform their radio show live and dress in character.

Using Book-Format and Other Graphic Organizers

Any type of three-dimensional, folded graphic organizer can be used with this activity. Students record a variety of information about vocabulary words as they appear in a reading passage: list the word, draw a picture, identify how it is used in the passage, and use it in a sentence (see Figure 47). Activities that cause students to reflect on a word in multiple ways may broaden their understanding. Also, having fun with unusual or quirky organizers like a paper airplane or a fan could breathe new life into an activity that has become routine.

Activities With Word Manipulatives

Students use manipulatives, such as magnetic words and plastic letter tiles, to construct vocabulary words (see Figure 48). Any type of manipulative can be used for this activity, which reinforces students' spelling and word-recognition skills. Students can incorporate technology and take photos of their work for display, or they can share their work with other groups.

Word-Game-Meister

Students construct their own game using the vocabulary list (see Figure 49), independently or in small groups. Once students begin working with words through the types of activities featured in this chapter, many develop a new appreciation for word games and activities. The "Word-Game-Meister" is designed for students who wish to craft their own word game, which could potentially become a new Literacy Bin Activity favorite. You might wish to incorporate students' use of various types of technology or include supplies to make new games.

Figure 49. Literacy Bin Activity Game Board Square for Word-Game-Meister

Create your own game using words from the vocabulary list. Be sure your game helps others learn the meaning of the words or helps others build their skills working with words.

Vocabulary and Word-Building Resource Materials

State and National Standards

In selecting your vocabulary words for inclusion in these activities, you may wish to access information from your state or national standards. For example, we accessed a link from our state education's website, where key ideas were featured for each grade level and within major content-based subject categories. These standards-based documents provide an additional level of specificity to learning standards, yet allow for creativity and interpretation to meet learners' needs. We reviewed these ideas as we selected key vocabulary words to include in our content lists.

State Assessments

Reviewing previous state assessments for keywords is another good source to consider as you compile your vocabulary lists. You might spot word variations or synonyms that did not appear in textbooks, state or national standards, or other sources you consult. Copies of former tests can often be accessed through state education websites, and your school district may also keep copies on file.

Textbook Selections

You will want to review your textbooks or other instructional materials to align and incorporate your keywords appearing in this material with vocabulary lists you prepare for the Literacy Bin Activities.

Books

Many good books are available on vocabulary and word-building skills. A selection of current works include the following:

- Allen, J. (1999). *Words, Words, Words: Teaching Vocabulary in Grades 4–12*. York, ME: Stenhouse.

- Baumann, J.F., & Kame'enui, E.J. (Eds.). (2004). *Vocabulary Instruction: Research to Practice*. New York: Guilford.

- Beck, I.L., McKeown, M.G., & Kucan, L. (2002). *Bringing Words to Life: Robust Vocabulary Instruction*. New York: Guilford.

- Beck, I.L., McKeown, M.G., & Kucan, L. (2008). *Creating Robust Vocabulary: Frequently Asked Questions and Extended Examples*. New York: Guilford.

- Blachowicz, C.L.Z., & Fisher, P. (2002). *Teaching Vocabulary in All Classrooms*. Upper Saddle River, NJ: Merrill/Prentice Hall.

- Block, C.C., & Mangieri, J.N. (2006). *The Vocabulary-Enriched Classroom: Practices for Improving the Reading Performance of All Students in Grades 3 and Up*. New York: Scholastic.

- Graves, M.F. (2006). *The Vocabulary Book: Learning and Instruction*. New York: Teachers College Press; Newark, DE: International Reading Association.

- Rasinski, T.V., Padak, N., Newton, R.M., & Newton, E. (2008). *Greek and Latin Roots: Keys to Building Vocabulary*. Huntington Beach, CA: Shell Education.

- Stahl, S.A., & Nagy, W.E. (2006). *Teaching Word Meanings*. Mahwah, NJ: Erlbaum.

Articles

Articles with supportive research that feature new instructional ideas for building students' vocabularies and word skills often appear in the publications of many professional organizations, such as the International Reading Association. You might wish to see which professional organizations your district belongs to and determine which periodicals and journals you can easily access. You might also wish to use an interlibrary loan system to access information.

Online Resources

There are many resources already available online that may be useful as you create your Literacy Bin Activities for building vocabulary knowledge and word skills.

- If your district uses a packaged spelling program, many make online activities available that align with your lessons. You might be able to incorporate some of these with your Literacy Bin Activities.
- Visit www.ReadWriteThink.org, which is a joint project of the International Reading Association and the National Council of Teachers of English, where you can explore many lessons that focus on vocabulary development and word skills.
- Many software programs are now available for educators to create traditional word games, such as word jumbles and crossword puzzles. Many of these can be accessed through a Google keyword search of *word games* and other similar phrases.
- You might also wish to access some of the general websites that feature teacher-created lesson plans, sites specializing in the use of specific technology, such as SMART board lessons, or some of the general educational websites that have game activities available. Some suggested sites include edhelper.com, atozteacherstuff.com, teachers.net/lessons/, and printables.scholastic.com.

Resources Used in Other Literacy Bin Activities

If some of your Literacy Bin Activities require the use of materials from your Literacy Bin Library, a collection of varied resource materials that can be used interchangeably with Literacy Bin Activities (see Chapter 1), you might wish to quickly review these materials for unusual variations or other new words or phrases that students may be exposed to. Some words appearing in these materials may not be used as widely as words from your textbook, yet would be useful in building in-depth word knowledge.

MOVING FORWARD

Although some types of activities in this chapter appear in other chapters, their emphasis here is to build vocabulary and word skills. For example, a drama activity used within this chapter, in which students dress in character and act out words, might appear similar to an activity in Chapter 5, in which students dramatize an event from history for the purpose of building their background knowledge. Still, the focus of each drama activity will be different, in keeping with the different instructional objectives. You may wish to keep this in mind as you develop your Literacy Bin's mix of activities if you do not want to include two drama activities (i.e., one to build vocabulary and the other to build background knowledge) in the same Literacy Bin. Instead, select activities that differ and collectively comprise a good mix, so students can select from a strong variety.

As repeated exposure to and practice with vocabulary and word activities is highly recommended by experts, including two or three of these in your Literacy Bin (even if the same vocabulary list is used) is appropriate. Select a good multimodal mix and include some that can be completed independently and in small groups. Also, many of the vocabulary and word-building activities could be adapted for use with multiple technologies. For example, word games could be modified using game programs within SMART board software and used independently, in small groups, or with the whole class.

If you have other literacy activities that your district requires or that will complement the way in which the Literacy Bins work, include them here. In addition to using the Literacy Bin Activities for developing students' content vocabulary, some teachers have incorporated general spelling or vocabulary word work along with the content activities recommended here. Some students may need supportive monitoring while working with these vocabulary and word-building activities. Monitoring methods can be adjusted according to students' needs and abilities (see Chapter 7).

Students often enjoy making their own word games. You might wish to include this as a swap activity. Consider ways to use these student-generated games as future activities.

CHAPTER 5

Activities to Construct Background Knowledge

As curriculum requirements become more rigorous and state testing and standards become more challenging, students and teachers need to meet the requirements or risk failure. If a student is promoted from grade to grade without mastering the content criteria for each level, the gap widens, and their struggle increases. Lenz (2005), of the University of Kansas Center for Research on Learning, suggests that "smarter" planning on the part of educators can increase content learning for students. Further, his research states "comprehension does not improve for students with limited content knowledge unless content area background knowledge is improved" (p. 10). One goal of the Literacy Bins is to improve content background knowledge and overall comprehension.

In our first year of teaching, we all learned the importance of relating new information to prior knowledge and scaffolding information to aid student understanding. Through the years, the curriculum has expanded, and we are trying to help our students connect more and more information. Yet this building of background knowledge is vital to the comprehension of content information. Students are constantly confronted with new information, particularly once they progress to the upper elementary grades. Their ability to grasp this information through their developing literacy skills is often taxed (Alexander, 2006). Assisting students by helping them build background knowledge works in a coordinated fashion with helping them develop their emerging and lifelong literacy skills. In fact, assisting them in building their knowledge while strengthening their skills was the impetus for our initial research into reading comprehension at the intermediate level (Athans & Devine, 2005).

In this chapter, we discuss the importance of constructing background knowledge and have highlighted key points stemming from research on the topic. We also share our own experiences in building background knowledge for our students. Then, we present Literacy Bin Activities and sample game board squares that you can use to enable students to construct background knowledge.

What Is Background Knowledge?

The terms *background knowledge*, *prior knowledge*, and even *domain knowledge* are often used interchangeably and generally mean what someone already knows about a given topic. Although some scholars describe prior knowledge more explicitly to mean the whole of a person's knowledge, including explicit and tacit knowledge, metacognitive and conceptual knowledge (Dochy & Alexander, 1995), the overall concept remains the same for most practitioners. Current research agrees that background knowledge is a vital component of reading comprehension.

Why Is Background Knowledge Important?

The link between background knowledge and comprehension is well established. One avenue that has contributed to our knowledge of this relationship is our understanding of schema theory, the "ways in which children connect the new to the known, recall relevant information, and enhance their comprehension" (Keene & Zimmermann, 2007, pp. 71–72). Today, we are all familiar with the need to activate students' prior knowledge, recognizing that they are more likely to retain and recall new information if it is linked or connected to their preexisting knowledge. To gain a clearer picture of the importance of this, some experts believe that students must understand roughly 90% of the words in a passage in order to comfortably construct enough meaning to figure out the remaining 10%. Moreover, "it's not just the words that the student has to grasp the meaning of—it's also the kind of reality that the words are referring to" (Hirsch, 2006, section II). Therefore, these findings ironically suggest that in order to become better at reading with understanding, students must already be able to read with understanding.

We are also aware of the need to scaffold our students' understandings, particularly as they encounter informational and content-rich passages within the curriculum. In today's classrooms, we routinely assist students by guiding and building their understandings. We provide essential details, translate complex events, and relate ideas to more commonly understood experiences. Our intent is that our students develop some degree of independence, so they can make meaning without relying on us. This gradual release of responsibility (Pearson & Fielding, 1996) has become routine in most classrooms today.

Last, we are all too well aware that reading comprehension is frequently a major focus of state and local testing and is one of the most common evaluation tools. High prior knowledge of a subject area or key vocabulary for a text often means higher test scores on reading comprehension measures (e.g., Langer, 1984; Long, Winograd, & Bridge, 1989; Stevens, 1980). Also, high correlations have been found between prior knowledge and speed and accuracy of study behavior (Dochy, Segers, & Buehl, 1999) as well as student interest in a topic (Tobias, 1994). So, whether we refer to it as *background knowledge*, *prior knowledge*, or *scaffolding*, the idea of linking new information to known has well-documented benefits. Background knowledge is important to all readers, young and old. It is what helps us connect and organize what we know and add new information to our repertoire of knowledge.

Our intent to conscientiously and wholeheartedly build our students' background knowledge was launched when we replaced several enjoyable fiction chapter books used within our literacy instruction with more content-related text. We had many skeptics at first. The works of fiction we replaced were well-established favorites, and the students and teachers enjoyed them. Still, we recognized that our students needed to develop deep understandings of complex topics in science and social studies. We also recognized that the 45-minute block of time we had traditionally allotted for this content instruction was insufficient. Double-dosing our students by using social studies and science materials in our reading instruction was a way we could help build their background knowledge *and* teach them to read.

Our curricular double-dosing seemed like it would be a win–win situation. Still, we were concerned that replacing some fiction favorites with texts about the Revolutionary War, immigration, and Thomas Edison's exploration of electrical circuits might not be viewed so favorably by other teachers and students. However, soon after the transition, our school librarian stopped in to tell us that in all her years as a school librarian, she had never seen anything like this and she wondered what had caused the change; the students were clamoring for more nonfiction books, especially on war, immigration, and Edison. In our attempt to use time more efficiently and build background knowledge, we were surprised by the added benefit of heightened student interest.

Since that time, we have built upon our collection of nonfiction, content-based materials that we use in our guided reading instruction. We have also learned how to support our students as they struggle to grasp difficult content concepts, and we have developed a familiarity with scaffolding their new knowledge so that they can situate it comfortably amidst something that is familiar and readily available to them when needed.

Our Literacy Bin Activities help reinforce the content we are teaching during our instruction, whether we are working with complex issues, such as war, immigration, slavery, or government, or if we are simply trying to build students' knowledge of story structure and genre. According to some literacy experts, the mainspring of comprehension is prior knowledge, which must in part come from a content-rich curriculum in school (Willingham, 2007).

Literacy Bin Activities to Enhance Background Knowledge

Students have a wide range of learning styles and rates of learning. Reading a text once and expecting that all students will comprehend and retain the information is not realistic, yet this happens in classrooms all the time. Teachers have so much material to cover in a short amount of time that it is difficult to give every subject sufficient coverage. Some content is expanded upon in each grade level as a child proceeds through school, and the repetition happens naturally. Although other subjects are instructed once, possibly from one chapter in a textbook and which may appear again on a test sometime in the future, the content may never really be understood by the student. By using content area materials for guided reading instruction, this information can be covered in two classes, thus giving the students more opportunity to interact with and learn the material. Adding Literacy Bins to the equation adds more opportunity for the student to review, practice, apply, and absorb new information. The following Literacy Bin

Activities add an expanded opportunity for students to gain content area information through a wide range of modalities.

Read at Home

Students sign out books on reserve at the library or from the book basket. These books offer information on the same topic, yet may present a different point of view or a new perspective. This activity can be adapted by varying the levels or length of reading passages. Reading can be done with a parent or other adult, or a student may read to another class (see Figure 50). This activity can be repeated with any topic and is a great way to offer students adult interaction and audience contact as well. The adult may simply listen to the student read or offer them further discussion on the topic to help establish connections and build background knowledge.

Figure 50. Literacy Bin Activity Game Board Square for Reading at Home

READ
Read at Home!

Sign out five different books or articles to read at home with your family. Have a parent sign your sheet and return it to school.

Create a Museum

Students select a person or event related to the current unit of study. They create a portrait, sculpture, or other art project, then write a narrative to display with it in a museum-type format (see Figure 51). This activity can incorporate technology, drama, and art and make use of materials you have readily available. You may repeat this activity using various themes to create an actual museum that students may walk through. They can also take photos and invite guests to attend. Alternatively, an online virtual museum can be saved electronically and visited all year. This activity is flexible and can easily be adjusted to fit class needs and curriculum goals.

Figure 51. Literacy Bin Activity Game Board Square for Creating a Museum

Colonial Times Museum
Help! Our museum needs more displays!

Create a portrait or sculpture of an event or person from Colonial times. Include a summary that has some important information about this person or event. Your work of art will be displayed in our Colonial Times Museum.

Glyphs

With this "self-portrait" activity (see Figure 52), students will follow a set of instructions, provided in the Literacy Bin (sample directions appear

Figure 52. Literacy Bin Activity Game Board Square for Glyphs

Create an eye-catching glyph about yourself!

A glyph is visual art where you can convey information about yourself. Your glyph will be about your experiences with topics we're learning in our immigration unit.

What a great way to make connections!

in Appendix A), to create a glyph, a piece of visual art that is used to convey meaning. In the example featured, students share information about themselves to coincide with the theme on immigration. They grasp issues about immigration by examining their own lives and heritage. Glyphs can be used for a variety of themes and in a variety of ways. Students often enjoy sharing their glyphs and discussing ideas about themselves. This is a popular activity and a great way to build background knowledge through connections.

Web Work

Students review several bookmarked websites related to the current theme. Sites can be found through an online search or recommended through teacher resource magazines or websites. It is important that all sites be reviewed by the teacher beforehand to ensure appropriate content. The

Figure 53. Literacy Bin Activity Game Board Square for Web Work

Did you know...?

Work with a partner or by yourself to search several government websites for 10 or more interesting facts to share with the class.

students will then record 10 new or interesting facts on a computer-based or paper note-taking page (see Figure 53). This activity allows the teacher to offer a wide range of related information to the class. Students will practice determining what information is most important or interesting to share. They can also practice taking notes or recording information electronically. We often find that students put extra effort into searching for unusual or offbeat facts.

Fact or Fiction? Card Game

Students sort several "fact or fiction?" cards into groups of true and false information (see Figure 54). Provide reference material for students to check their work. As a bonus, you can provide some blank cards for students to create some of their own. This activity encourages students to use reference materials to check facts and to analyze information to create their own questions. Students can complete this activity independently, with a partner, or in small groups, either working collaboratively or by taking turns.

Create a Slideshow

Students create a slideshow presentation on the current unit of study (see Figure 55). A planning page to organize important information may be provided. The amount of planning and writing may be adjusted to meet your goals. Many students are motivated by using technology or creating something to present to others. It is also great for students of this age to practice and expand their computer skills. The final project may be shared with classmates, schoolwide, or with the community. This project may incorporate a wide range of research, note-taking, technology, speaking, and listening skills.

Perform a Readers Theatre Script

Students practice and perform a Readers Theatre script based on the current unit of study (see Figure 56). By organizing roles and reviewing scripts, students will gain insights into the topic. This is a very popular activity that can be repeated with each new theme. Readers Theatre scripts can be published material or you (or the students) can write your own. Students often like to create props to use during their performance. This, too, supports the development of their background knowledge.

Figure 54. Literacy Bin Activity Game Board Square for the Fact or Fiction? Card Game

Fact or Fiction?

Sort the "fact or fiction?" cards into two groups: true and false. Use the books from the Literacy Bin to check any that you are unsure of.

Bonus: Use the books to find information to create your own "fact or fiction?" cards to add to our game.

Figure 55. Literacy Bin Activity Game Board Square for Creating a Slideshow

HOME STATE SLIDESHOW

Complete a planning page with information about your home state. Use this information to create a PowerPoint presentation.

Figure 56. Literacy Bin Activity Game Board Square for Performing a Readers Theatre Script

Erie Canal Readers Theatre

Practice reading "Night on the Erie Canal" with your group. When your group is ready, sign up for a time to present to the class.

Figure 57. Literacy Bin Activity Game Board Square for Postcard From...

Figure 58. Literacy Bin Activity Game Board Square for Creating a Rap

Figure 59. Literacy Bin Activity Game Board Square for Comic Book Writer

Postcard From...

Students write a postcard from a time and place that coincides with the theme of the Literacy Bin (see Figure 57). They can even assume the role of a historic figure or character. Providing students with resources to use within the Literacy Bin will help them capture the essence of the period. Students can illustrate a side of their postcard, testing their knowledge of the times by thinking about the historical accuracy of their ideas and images. Students might wish to make a postcard mobile so that both sides of their postcard will show. As another variation, students might wish to correspond with one another as if role-playing in that time period.

Create a Rap

Students practice and perform a musical rap (or any other type of music) based on the current unit of study (see Figure 58). Students can use classroom resources to gather information to write their music. This activity can be done in collaboration with the music teacher. This format of reading, creating, and performing may appeal to some students who may be reluctant or struggle with other modalities of instruction. Likewise, there are many technology-based programs that allow students to record and enhance this activity.

Comic Book Writer

Students may work alone or with a group to create a comic strip or comic book about a theme, such as life on the Erie Canal (see Figure 59). They should include text and illustrations. The style of research and sharing of information offers a creative and artistic mode for students to build background knowledge. The finished product can be shared with the class or put on display. You may want to provide a variety of art materials and samples of completed comic books for students to use. Another popular format that could be used with this activity is the graphic novel. Here, students can create nonfiction mininovels that include comic-like renditions of people, places, and events, similar to the style used in popular graphic novels.

Mock Trial

Students conduct a mock trial and determine the guilt or innocence of a historical figure or a character from literature (see Figure 60). You can provide them with main topics to debate and let them conduct research using materials from the Literacy Bin. Alternatively, you can have students devise the topic of the trial based on specific resources you provide in the Literacy Bin compartment. A variation on this activity is to have students debate a topic related to the Literacy Bin theme. They can debate any number of topics, from the most influential explorer to the most extraordinary tall tale character. Students can work in pairs or teams for their debate or trial. Learning significant facts and details about their topic will help build their background knowledge.

Figure 60. Literacy Bin Activity Game Board Square for a Mock Trial

Guilty or Innocent?
That Is the Question!

Using a sheet from the Literacy Bin, select a questionable issue surrounding Christopher Columbus's journey and exploration of the New World. Based on facts and details you learn from resources in the Literacy Bin, determine who is guilty or innocent in the issue you select.

Craft a RAFT

The RAFT strategy (Santa, 1988)—role, audience, format, and topic—offers students a creative outlet for demonstrating understanding. Students communicate information by taking an unusual point of view and writing for a specific audience. With "Craft a RAFT," students write about a well-known topic or subject related to the theme of the Literacy Bin (see Figure 61). The sample figure is used within a Literacy Bin on

Figure 61. Literacy Bin Activity Game Board Square for Creating a RAFT

GREEK MYTHOLOGY RAFT

Create a RAFT about the well-known story of Persephone and her harrowing adventures! Follow the guidelines in the Literacy Bin.

Ancient Greece (see Appendix A for sample directions). While crafting a RAFT, students can manipulate their knowledge about a story or event to turn it into a creative new form of expression. Students will have to grasp ideas well before they are able to reshape them into a RAFT. Students might wish to work in pairs. Students can be directed to work with a textbook (if available) or materials in the Literacy Bin, or you may wish to provide them with specific resources.

ABC Bookmark

Students make an oversized ABC bookmark with alphabet letters using phrases or key ideas from their unit (see Figure 62). Students might be instructed to hunt through resources provided in the Literacy Bin compartment, the Literacy Bin Library, or a textbook. They can also devise their own sentences or phrases connected to the theme. Encouraging students to consider everything they know and build on their knowledge through these types of creative connections is one way to strengthen this skill. Students can color their bookmark to make the sequence of letters stand out. They can also share their ideas with others by presenting their bookmark or displaying it in the classroom.

Figure 62. Literacy Bin Activity Game Board Square for ABC Bookmarks

ABC Bookmark

Never lose your place in your studies of electrical circuits! Craft an ABC bookmark by devising short sentences, key ideas, and pithy sayings about electricity. Share with a friend!

Background Knowledge–Related Resource Materials

Information on background knowledge can be found within many general works on literacy improvement, although there are many resources specifically focused on building background knowledge. You might also wish to review ideas on scaffolding, which is a topic linked to the development of background knowledge. Specific recommendations are outlined in this section.

State and National Standards

As mentioned in other chapters, it is helpful to review and use your state or national standards as a guide while creating background-knowledge activities. For example, there may be key indicators that will provide some specificity to clarify the depth and scope of knowledge that students are expected to learn. Likewise, you might find some clever ideas that will help you shape activities offered in this chapter or create your own.

Activities within this chapter support many standards by encouraging students to explore additional information on topics that align with many grade-level curricula. Students are encouraged to evaluate and manipulate what they have read to create materials or complete activities, thus helping them to scaffold what they have learned into their background knowledge.

Books

Many good books are available on building background knowledge. A selection of current works include the following:

- Keene, E.O., & Zimmermann, S. (2007). *Mosiac of Thought: The Power of Comprehension Strategy Instruction*. Portsmouth, NH, Heinemann.

- Marzano, R.J. (2004). *Building Background Knowledge for Academic Achievement: Research on What Works in Schools*. Alexandria, VA: Association for Supervision and Curriculum Development.

- McEwan, E.K. (2007). *Use Easy Nonfiction to Build Background Knowledge*. Retrieved July 14, 2009, from www.AdLit.org/article/19865

- Zimmermann, S., & Hutchins, C. (2003). *7 Keys to Comprehension: How to Help Your Kids Read It and Get It!* New York: Three Rivers Press.

Articles

If you or your district belongs to professional organizations, such as the International Reading Association, you may wish to search their periodicals for current information on fluency and related topics. In many cases, articles can be downloaded free of charge or for a small fee.

Online Resources

Using search engines and keywords and phrases, such as *background knowledge*, *prior knowledge*, and *content* or *domain knowledge*, will help narrow your search for further information. Other keywords that may lead to helpful searches include *scaffolding* or *connections*. Reviewing the well-known gradual release of responsibility model might also be helpful.

MOVING FORWARD

Background knowledge can be enhanced by reading supplemental material or researching related, similar, or even contradictory information about the subject matter. Varying perspectives and added information will help students gain insight and form opinions.

Often schools are provided with basic resources to provide content area instruction. To help your students gain background knowledge, you may need to search for supplemental materials. Your school or public library will have further reading material on most topics, and websites may offer more ideas and information. Collecting newspaper articles and magazines may also be valuable.

Allowing the students some opportunities to research a topic independently, while collaborating with peers for other activities, will also aid their ability to gain new insights and perspectives. Often we find that students modify their initial thoughts and opinions on content area topics once they have completed some Literacy Bin Activities designed to build background knowledge.

CHAPTER 6

Activities to Develop Fluency

Once referred to as "the neglected goal" of reading education (Allington, 1983), fluency has attracted a great deal of attention since its inclusion in the Report of the National Reading Panel (NICHD, 2000). At that time, fluency had been identified as one of five critical pillars for reading success. In response to these early initiatives, many teachers began monitoring their students' rate of reading, calculating the number of words each student could read per minute, then setting improvement goals based on general guidelines created by literacy specialists (e.g., Fountas & Pinnell, 2001; Hasbrouck & Tindal, 1992). Although well-intentioned, these actions resulted in concerns among practitioners, researchers, and specialists alike, who cautioned that too much emphasis was placed on word rate alone and not on other factors that affected fluency and comprehension. As a result of these early findings, we now have new guidelines that steer us toward a more effective approach to fluency instruction. There is no doubt that fluency should remain in the spotlight, for its relationship to comprehension is well documented. There is also no doubt that our early false starts have better equipped us to make significant gains with our students' fluency today.

In this chapter, you will learn about key issues that literacy specialists have explored in their research on fluency. You will also grasp how the fluency activities designed for use in your Literacy Bins can complement your literacy instruction. Finally, you can review a vast and varied collection of fun-tastic activities for developing your students' fluency skills.

What Is Fluency?

Although there are some differing interpretations among leading experts today, most agree that reading fluency refers to the ability of readers to read "quickly, effortlessly, and efficiently with good, meaningful expression" (Rasinski, 2003, p. 26). Clearly, fluency has incorporated a much larger focus on proficiencies that extend beyond word count; for example, *oral reading, intonation, punctuation*, and *pacing* are categories appearing within a well-known oral reading fluency rubric (Applegate, Quinn, & Applegate, 2008). Meanwhile, rate, phrasing, intonation, pausing, and stress—and the integration of all five—are among those critical factors identified by others (Fountas & Pinnell, 2006). The role of prosody in fluency has recently gained momentum and is defined as the emphasis or stress, pitch or intonation, tempo, and rhythm that captures the authenticity of speaking while reading (e.g., Harris & Hodges, 1995; Zutell & Rasinski, 1991). Table 5 features some measurement devices with a selection of the well-known words-per-minute rate guidelines.

Why Is Fluency Important?

Reading fluency is important, because it contributes greatly to reading comprehension. Experts contend that if a student's focus and attention is consumed with reading individual words, there may be little left to attend to comprehension (LaBerge & Samuels, 1974). Rasinski (2003) refers to this as "cognitive effort" (p. 35) and further notes that once this cognitive effort is freed up from the task of making sense of individual words, comprehension improves. The way to do this is by building students' oral reading abilities.

From our own research with fluency (Athans, Devine, Henry, & Sammon, 2007), we discovered that fluent readers often had to practice their fluency as they read new and unfamiliar passages in science and social studies. Different stumbling blocks, such as content vocabulary or maneuvering through a double-column format, tripped up fluent readers as they plodded through informational and content-based reading passages. They also struggled to make sense of unusual features, such as excerpts or direct quotations that represented words spoken by historical figures. New content-based concepts also affected the way in which the readers read aloud their own written thoughts. We were concerned about this for our otherwise fluent readers, yet we also recognized the problem would be even worse for our students whose fluency was taxed by general reading passages. Our findings are supported by others; for example, according to Brozo and Flynt (2008), "content text requires greater effort to process and understand.... The less time students spend engaged with content

Table 5. Words-per-Minute Fluency Guidelines

Hasbrouck and Tindal Oral Reading Fluency Data: 50th Percentile

Grade Level	Fall WCPM	Winter WCPM	Spring WCPM
2	51	72	89
3	71	92	107
4	94	112	123
5	110	127	139
6	127	140	150

Note. WCPM = words correct per minute. Hasbrouck and Tindal recommend that students falling below 50% should receive a fluency-building program. Adapted from J.E. Hasbrouck & G. Tindal, 2006, 2006 Hasbrouck & Tindal Oral Reading Fluency Data, St. Paul, MN: Read Naturally, retrieved October 15, 2009, from www.readnaturally.com/pdf/oralreadingfluency.pdf

Fountas and Pinnell's Oral Reading Rates

Grade Level	Range (Words per Minute)
2	80–100
3	100–120
4	120–145
5	145–170
6	170–190

Note. Adapted from I.C. Fountas & G.S. Pinnell, 2006, *Teaching for Comprehending and Fluency: Thinking, Talking, and Writing About Reading, K–8*, p. 71, Portsmouth, NH: Heinemann.

Reading A–Z's Recommendations

Grade Level	Early WCPM	End WCPM
2	70	100
3	100	130
4	130	140
5	140	160
6	160	170

Note. WCPM = words correct per minute. Adapted from Reading A–Z, n.d., Fluency Standards Table: Recommendations, retrieved October 15, 2009, from www.readinga-z.com/fluency/index.html

Rasinski's Oral Fluency Rates

Grade Level	Rate
2	90
3	110
4	140
5	150
6	180

Note. From T.V. Rasinski, 2003, *The Fluent Reader: Oral Reading Strategies for Building Word Recognition, Fluency, and Comprehension*, p. 80, New York: Scholastic.

area text the more underdeveloped their reading skills will be for this type of material" (p. 172). Clearly, students benefit from additional experiences with content literacy activities, including those that are targeted to strengthen content fluency.

We also found that readers who struggled with fluency were often at a strong disadvantage with content-based literature as they struggled to grasp other clues, such as morphemic, syntactic, semantic, and pragmatic clues, that might otherwise aid their fluency and comprehension. In addition, searching for time-saving shortcuts to reduce the repeated practice that is key in helping to strengthen student fluency may be misguided. Instead, providing appealing activities that students want to practice repeatedly may prove more effective.

Engaging students with enjoyable passages for repeated readings is key (Stanley, 2004). Today, practitioners can select from an assortment of ways in which to incorporate meaningful fluency instruction and practice into their reading program, from telling jokes (Ness, 2009) to performing Readers Theatre scripts that incorporate movement (Peebles, 2007). All of the activities presented in this chapter are developed with this guiding principle in mind. We also were careful to craft "fluency-rich activities," ones that would enable students to practice multiple facets of fluency in "an integrated and synergistic manner" (Rasinski, 2006, p. 705). Teachers could monitor students' words-per-minute rate (if they chose) and also easily note gains in other, equally important areas, such as prosody. As Rasinski makes clear, reading for meaning must be emphasized, and this can be accomplished by providing students with activities such as poetry, songs, chants, rhymes, monologues, dialogues, and letters, which encourage students' expressive oral performance.

However, we must be mindful of the many studies that remind us that fluency alone cannot be used to evaluate students' reading proficiency without regard for comprehension (Applegate, Applegate, & Modla, 2009; Rasinski, 2006). We have all witnessed in our classes those students who can read fluently, with good speed, phrasing, and prosody, yet cannot grasp meaning. The interrelationship between fluency and comprehension is a complex one that should not be oversimplified. As building student fluency remains one objective among others within your Literacy Bin Activities, we intend to address this caution.

Literacy Bin Activities to Develop Fluency

The Literacy Bin Activities presented in this chapter are examples of ideas you could use to develop student fluency. Many of the activities may also help meet other objectives, such as constructing background knowledge or building vocabulary or word skills (and may appear in those chapters, too), yet their emphasis here is on developing fluency skills. A general description of each activity and suggestions for ways in which it could be modified are provided. Information you might wish to place in the Literacy Bin compartment, such as instructions or student materials, are also listed. Use the activities featured here, modify them as you wish, or create your own using these models. As you review the activities, you might also consider materials you have available or can readily locate to use with the activities.

Perform a Readers Theatre Script

Students select a script to practice and perform in front of the class (see Figure 63). Students might wish to add simple props that can be made with easily accessible materials. This activity can be performed by a

small group or independently, depending on the materials you use as a script. You can use commercial scripts or create your own from classroom resources. You may wish to attach a brief set of guidelines to the scripts to remind students about reading for expression and accuracy, which will alert them to the importance of reading punctuation and other text clues that will help them make meaning. It will also encourage their repeated practice of tricky words or phrases often found in informational passages.

Figure 63. Literacy Bin Activity Game Board Square for Performing a Readers Theatre Script

Casting Call
for all
Drama Queens & Kings!
Select one of the scripts and practice, practice, practice your lines until you can deliver them perfectly! You may create simple props. Be prepared to deliver a flawless performance for your classmates.

Recite Poetry

Students select or write a poem to recite aloud (see Figure 64). This activity can incorporate movement and be performed in small groups using shared or multiple-voice poems. Poems that include alliteration, rhyme, or

Figure 64. Literacy Bin Activity Game Board Square for Reciting Poetry

Poetry Palooza!

Dazzle your friends,
amaze your classmates,
and show off your expert skill!

Select a poem from the Literacy Bin and
practice reciting it until it's Poetry
Palooza perfect. Then perform it!

Figure 65. Literacy Bin Activity Game Board Square for Read-Aloud Storytelling

Master Storyteller

Select a book from the Literacy Bin Library
and practice reading it several times. As a
Master Storyteller, you must read with
expression, good pacing, and expert
pronunciation. You may wish to read it to a
friend before reading it aloud to the class.

Figure 66. Literacy Bin Activity Game Board Square for Performing a Speech

Speech

Select one of the famous
speeches from the Literacy
Bin. You should practice
reading the speech aloud
and using expression that
captures the emotions
of the original.

assonance will help build students' articulation skills and are fun to perform. Poems can be created on any topic and may even take the form of a RAFT (see Chapter 5), a popular literacy tool that can be used flexibly within content areas. Students can be assigned a role, audience, format, and topic (i.e., the letters comprising the acronym RAFT) that support the theme of the Literacy Bin. Repeated readings of the RAFT will help students build fluency skills.

Read-Aloud Storytelling

Students choose a passage or book from the Literacy Bin Library. Then, they can assume the role of a featured author, time traveler, clairvoyant, or another character appropriate for the Literacy Bin theme while delivering their read-aloud (see Figure 65). In this "Master Storyteller" activity, students are encouraged to monitor many of their fluency skills. You might want students to focus on one area at a time, such as reading punctuation, especially at the lower elementary levels. Building students' skills in other areas, such as content automaticity (i.e., reading content vocabulary words fluently) could be reserved for subsequent Literacy Bins. Using technology to record or present their read-aloud can strengthen the appeal of this activity.

Perform a Speech

Students select a text from the Literacy Bin and present it in front of the class as a speech (see Figure 66). You may wish to include famous speeches, passages from letters, or other documents that align with the theme of your Literacy Bin. Well-known passages may be readily available or require minimal time to locate. For example, kid-friendly versions of the U.S. Constitution are easily accessible on the Internet. Alternately, students can write the thoughts or feelings of a character. Encouraging students to work in pairs or small groups might be a way to help nonfluent readers build their skills. Partners could provide positive feedback and model appropriate expression and emotion.

Sing a Song

Students practice the words to thematic-based songs and perform in front of the class (see Figure 67). Locating an audio version of the song is often helpful for students. Alternately, they may enjoy musical accompaniment if working with your music teacher is an option. Encouraging students to write their own verses using popular tunes is a variation of this activity. For example, younger elementary students could write and perform a song about animal habitats using the format and tune of "The Itsy-Bitsy Spider." Older students could write and perform a song about the Roman Empire to the tune of "Happy Birthday." Encouraging students to include content vocabulary or to repeat verses (i.e., create a chorus) will help build their fluency skills. You might also use technology to record and present this activity.

Figure 67. Literacy Bin Activity Game Board Square for Singing a Song

LOW BRIDGE, EVERYBODY DOWN!

Singers and songwriters wanted!

Sing this popular canal song with some of your friends and write new verses that capture your knowledge of the times.

Present a Monologue or Soliloquy

Students select an individual to study and prepare a self-reflective passage in character (see Figure 68). This activity can be used in a variety of ways. Students can demonstrate personality traits of a well-known character, such as the wolf in the fairy tale "The Three Little Pigs." Other students might want to assume the role of a recognized individual and lament the struggles he or she faced, such as

Figure 68. Literacy Bin Activity Game Board Square for Presenting a Monologue or Soliloquy

In The Spotlight
In The Spotlight

Select a character from this period of time and put them in the spotlight. What feelings, thoughts, and ideas might they wish to share with others, or speak aloud when they thought no one was listening? Using materials from the Literacy Bin Library, select a character and write and present a one-paragraph "think bubble" that best captures what they're all about.

Abraham Lincoln, who struggled with the conflicts between the North and South. Encouraging students to capture and share feelings and thoughts will help them grasp the importance of expression. Students can perform individually or create a scene and have other characters freeze on stage while delivering their script. Helping students identify significant people, places, and events is often all that's needed to get them started.

Puppet Shows

Students decide on an event for a puppet show and prepare a brief script to deliver (see Figure 69). They can create simple paper puppets from easily accessible materials like paper plates attached to a wooden paint stirrer or brown bags that can be worn as masks. Although the example in Figure 69 references a historic time period, its format is flexible and can be used for many themes. You may wish to provide some suggested people and events for students the first time you use this activity. Encourage them to work on the delivery of their brief script, because the area of focus is to build fluency. Audio and digital technology can easily be used with this activity.

Figure 69. Literacy Bin Activity Game Board Square for Puppet Shows

Looking for Skilled Puppeteers!

Create a brief skit of a significant event from this time period and perform it using puppets. Practice, practice, practice your lines, so you can deliver them flawlessly. Puppets can be constructed from art materials in the cabinet.

Sign of the Times

With this activity, students use a blab sheet—a teacher-prepared sheet based on a recitation practice used during the first decade of the 20th century in "blab schools." A common practice for those times, students memorized and recited assigned reading passages. For this activity, students will recite their content-based passages in front of peers (see Figure 70). You may wish to encourage students to practice with an audio recording device, so they can work toward improving their fluency skills. Another version of this activity is to encourage students to perform their recitations and then conduct a lesson for their classmates.

Figure 70. Literacy Bin Activity Game Board Square for Sign of the Times

A Blab School?

Abraham Lincoln attended a Blab School where he and his classmates practiced reciting their lessons at the very same time.

Blab...blab...blab!

Select a buddy or two and recreate a scene from a Blab School. You may use one of the recitation scripts provided in the Literacy Bin or create one of your own. Remember that recitations were practiced repeatedly!

Blab, Blab, Blab School!

Finger and Movement Rhymes

A finger rhyme is an activity reminiscent of long ago, and although it is often used to accompany popular children's nursery rhymes, it can also be used here to help students build fluency. As outlined in the activity "Clap, Snap, and Hop!" students select a passage from the Literacy Bin and add sound effects or movements (see Figure 71). Well-known passages may be readily available or require minimal time to locate. Encouraging students to identify word phrases and recognize language rhythms through punctuation will help them build their fluency skills. This activity also works well with poetry and with passages that include language or expressions unique to a historical period or genre, such as tall tale passages, which typically use unfamiliar idioms or unusual words or phrases. Alternatively, students can write their own material. Students may wish to present this activity using audiovisual technologies.

Figure 71. Literacy Bin Activity Game Board Square for Finger and Movement Rhymes

Clap, Snap, and Hop!

Add some rhythm to a well-known speech or passage by performing it with a little *razz-a-ma-tazz!*

Select a passage from the Literacy Bin, practice reading it aloud, then perform it with sound effects or movement. Enhance the natural rhythm of the language with some *razz-a-ma-tazz!*

Imaginative Challenges

Students select a sheet of phrases from the Literacy Bin, practice reading them, then perform for the class with 100% accuracy as if they are a human echo chamber (see Figure 72). One student recites a phrase and the other repeats it back perfectly. Phrases used for this activity can be linked to a character or event in your themed Literacy Bin. For example, providing biographical details on Henry Hudson for a theme on explorers could help students tackle hard-to-master content vocabulary. Also, reciting common rules of spelling could be used for a general back-to-school Literacy Bin. Directions should encourage students to read with the same prosody. Students might wish to write phrases or accept challenges from their audience. They might also wish to make a simple prop to represent the echo chamber.

Figure 72. Literacy Bin Activity Game Board Square for Imaginative Challenges

HUMAN ECHO... ECHO... ECHO... CHAMBER

You and your partner have accepted the challenge of becoming a human echo chamber. Using your sheet of phrases from the Literacy Bin, read a passage into the chamber and make it echo back perfectly. PRACTICE... PRACTICE... PRACTICE...

Imaginative Characters

Using an unpunctuated passage from the Literacy Bin, students restore the punctuation and meaning while pretending to be an imaginative character called "The Punctu-ator." First, they restore the punctuation to the paper copy, then perform the corrected version in front of the class (see Figure 73). Students can work independently or in pairs. Encouraging them to practice reading the passage before reading it aloud to the class will help them reflect on the accuracy of their punctuation. It will also enable them to grasp the importance of the use of punctuation, especially as it affects numerous components of fluency. As an alternative, you might want students to record their reading using an audio device.

Figure 73. Literacy Bin Activity Game Board Square for Imaginative Characters

The Punctu-ator

You are The Punctu-ator, skilled at placing proper punctuation in passages, so meaning can be restored!

Restore the proper punctuation to the passage in the Literacy Bin, practice reading it, then deliver it with expression to your admiring fans!

Canon Sing-Along

Students write and perform a round with two friends on topics aligned with the Literacy Bin theme. You may suggest that students use tunes from any of the popular rounds (canons), such as "Row, Row, Row Your Boat," as a way to easily begin this activity (see Figure 74). As many of the verses repeat, students should be encouraged to practice phrasing and incorporate tricky ideas that may include difficult vocabulary words, such as phrases like *electricity follows the path of least resistance* for a themed Literacy Bin on electricity. Students tend to welcome these challenges if they are placed within a comfortable framework of a familiar canon. Encouraging them to work on their rhythm and articulation to help build fluency.

Figure 74. Literacy Bin Activity Game Board Square for Canon Sing-Along

Row, Row, Row Your Boat
Row, Row, Row Your Boat
Row, Row, Row Your Boat

Find two friends and write a song about the arrival of the colonists in the New World. Verses should be informative and accurate. Practice, practice, practice, then perform your song in a round. Use materials from the Literacy Bin Library and your reading materials.

Fantasy Activities

Students create a PowerPoint on topics they've studied that align with the Literacy Bin theme using their reading materials or materials from the Literacy Bin Library. "Alien Tour Guide" is the perfect backdrop for students to share their fluency skills on a variety of content-based themes (see Figure 75). Although the Erie Canal is the one used in the example, many different themes will work, such as penguins, explorers, seasons, simple machines, and industrialization. Being able to present content information fluently is the hallmark of a good tour guide and the challenge students accept when they choose this activity. Students should be versed in creating slideshows and performing Internet searches, so they can create these independently. Classmates can assume the roles of alien students and ask questions.

Congratulations! You and a buddy have been selected to be tour guides for a group of alien students who will be visiting our school. Make an electronic "knowledge gallery" on the Erie Canal using PowerPoint and explain the who, what, when, where, and why of your slides in a well-rehearsed presentation. Have fun!

Imaginative Games

Students select passages from the Literacy Bin and demonstrate how to deliver a passage with expression, pacing, and articulation. "What a Great Imposter!" is a fun-tastic game in which students practice their fluency skills by impersonating a famous person from the past (see Figure 76). Early elementary students could choose from well-known storybook characters, such as Charlotte in *Charlotte's Web*. For older students, historic figures, such as U.S. presidents, Civil Rights leaders, and influential women, could be used, depending upon the theme of your Literacy Bin. You might want students to select from three or four different passages provided in the Literacy Bin compartment, or students might wish to create their own passage. This can become very comical, depending upon the tone adopted by presenters.

Figure 76. Literacy Bin Activity Game Board Square for Imaginative Games

What a Great Imposter!

You are training your partner to deliver lines just like a famous person from this time period would have delivered them. Instruct your partner on expression, pacing, and articulation, so s/he can be

a great imposter!

Cheers

Students select a passage, speech, or informational text and use it to create a cheer (see Figure 77). Students should be encouraged to include expression and might wish to add movements, as in the "Rah! Rah! Rah!"

Figure 77. Literacy Bin Activity Game Board Square for Cheers

Rah! Rah! Rah!

Select a passage from the Literacy Bin and create a cheer for it. Be sure to use sections of the passage in your cheer. You may also wish to add some "rah! rah! rah!" movements to rally the audience! Practice your cheer, so you can deliver it accurately...and *cheerfully!*

example. To encourage students to practice fluency skills, select passages that pose challenges and ask students to incorporate tricky sections in their cheers. Allowing students to explore different volumes while delivering their cheers could be a treat and a dramatic departure from their other fluency-building activities. Students can also explore a twist by presenting their cheer through choral reading or in other creative ways.

Jump Rope Jingles and Routines

Students select a content-based passage and perform it to the rhythm of the jump rope (see Figure 78). You might wish to have students practice reading the passage during class time and work on the jump roping outside at recess. Blending the natural rhythms of the activity with the delivery of the content-based jingle could help some students improve fluency challenges, such as pacing. You might also work collaboratively with the physical education teacher to schedule additional time for this activity. Students can work in pairs or in small teams.

Figure 78. Literacy Bin Activity Game Board Square for Jump Rope Jingles and Routines

Jumpers, Grab Your Ropes!

Use a passage from the Literacy Bin to create a jump rope routine or jingle to go along with it! You can take turns with a friend and have them jump while you read, then switch places. Or you can come up with another way to perform your passage using the natural rhythm of jump roping.

Simulations and Dramatic Play

Students select a thematic passage from the Literacy Bin and read it into the "articulation simulation machine." The student who is role-playing the machine reads it back using perfect articulation (see Figure 79). In this zany activity, students can "ham it up" and demonstrate how phrasing, intonation, volume, and pitch can be improved by the articulation simulation machine. Students can read passages either sentence-by-sentence or in short paragraphs. They can also take turns, so each gets a chance

Figure 79. Literacy Bin Activity Game Board Square for Simulations and Dramatic Play

The Amazing Articulation Simulation Machine!

You and a buddy just invented an amazing "articulation simulation machine" and wish to demonstrate how it works to your classmates. Select a passage from the Literacy Bin and read it into the machine. Dazzle your friends as they listen to the machine deliver a perfectly articulated version of it!

to practice articulation skills. Students can add a machine prop, such as by decorating a desk with construction paper or using a study carrel that features a picture of an imaginative machine.

How-To Demonstrations

Students select a passage from the Literacy Bin and take turns demonstrating how to read it using good fluency skills (see Figure 80). The "How-To Demonstration" featured in the example can be used for a variety of themes. Students might wish to include props, such as posters, that include critical factors. They might also invite the audience to try out the skills they're demonstrating. Including their own "tips" on ways to improve fluency is something else students might be encouraged to share with others. Last, students often want to create their own content material, having recognized and overcome their own struggles with cumbersome content issues.

Figure 80. Literacy Bin Activity Game Board Square for How-To Demonstrations

Fluency Facts:
A How-To Demonstration

You and a partner(s) will perform a "fluency facts how-to" by demonstrating five critical ways to make reading fluent. Select a passage from the Literacy Bin to demonstrate expression, articulation, pacing, phrasing, and volume.

Timing Activities

"On Your Mark" is an activity that asks students to consider their word count per minute. Students time their reading using a timing device and a passage from the Literacy Bin (see Figure 81). As cautioned earlier in this chapter, this is only one component of fluency. Numerous other fluency activities presented here focus on other components. Still, this is a favorite. When reviewing this activity during the introduction of your Literacy Bin, you might want to clarify that accuracy and comprehension are as important as the number of words that can be read. You might suggest students work in pairs or in small groups. Providing a suggested time-length goal within an appropriate range should discourage students from reading too quickly. Students can record their reading or perform in front of the class.

Figure 81. Literacy Bin Activity Game Board Square for Timing Activities

On Your Mark...
Get Set...
and Time Yourself!

Use the timer in the Literacy Bin to see if you can improve your pace reading the passage. Remember that you must read with expression and accuracy. Practice, practice, and practice some more!

Figure 82. Literacy Bin Activity Game Board Square for Advice Activities

> ### fluency "fix-Ups" With Dr. flabbergast
> **Have a blast pretending to fix common fluency errors by following the advice of the zany doctor!**
>
> Use the passage provided in the Literacy Bin to focus your improvement activities on five critical skills that will aid fluency.

Advice Activities

Students use passages in the Literacy Bin to demonstrate typical problems with fluency and offer fix-up advice. Students can work in pairs or small groups and use an interview or letter format during their performance (see Figure 82). They might also wish to add props and dress in character to assume the role of "Dr. Flabbergast."

Fluency-Related Resource Materials

State and National Standards

In addition to reviewing the activities presented in this chapter, we also encourage you to review your state or national standards to help you devise sound fluency activities. Guidelines provided for standards may include key indicators, which can provide reassurance that your activities align with the literacy standards. You might also find that your state education department may suggest other good, standards-based ideas, which can help steer you as you create your own activities or even as you modify some of those presented within this chapter.

Activities within this chapter not only support fluency development through choral and repeated readings, among other strategies suggested by educational experts, but also align with many standards. Staying on top of changes made to your state or national standards will also ensure that your literacy activities are current.

Books

The following books are good resources that can provide you with more information about fluency. Many have been written by the literacy experts cited in the chapter.

- Allington, R.L. (2009). *What Really Matters in Fluency: Research-Based Practices Across the Curriculum*. Boston: Allyn & Bacon/ Pearson.

- Fountas, I.C., & Pinnell, G.S. (2006). *Teaching for Comprehending and Fluency: Thinking, Talking, and Writing About Reading, K–8.* Portsmouth, NH: Heinemann.

- Fountas, I.C., & Pinnell, G.S. (2008). *Fountas & Pinnell Benchmark Assessment System 2: Assessment Guide.* Portsmouth, NH: Heinemann.

- Pressley, M., Gaskins, I., & Fingeret, L. (2006). Instruction and Development of Reading Fluency in Struggling Readers. In S.J. Samuels & A.E. Farstrup (Eds.), *What Research Has to Say About Fluency Instruction* (pp. 47–69). Newark, DE: International Reading Association.

- Rasinski, T.V. (2003). *The Fluent Reader: Oral Reading Strategies for Building Word Recognition, Fluency, and Comprehension.* New York: Scholastic.

- Rasinski, T., Fry, E., & Knoblock, K. (2007). *Increasing Fluency With High Frequency Word Phrases Grade 2.* Huntington Beach, CA: Shell Education. (*Note:* The authors have written these texts for grades 3–5 as well.)

Articles

If you or your district belongs to professional organizations, such as the International Reading Association, you may wish to search their periodicals for current information on fluency and related topics. In many cases, articles can be downloaded free of charge or for a small fee.

Online Resources

Using search engines and keywords, such as *fluency* and *prosody*, will narrow your search for further information that may be helpful.

MOVING FORWARD

Most of the fluency activities enable you to use audio and visual technologies. Depending on your available resources and your own comfort level using the technologies, you may wish to incorporate them into these

Literacy Bin Activities. Working together with your technology specialist may be helpful.

Some of the fluency activities specifically address ways in which to improve fluency, while others assume a subtler approach to fluency improvement. In our experience, both types work well and are another way to offer students variety. You will want to be certain that any terminology you use in your activity description is clear to students. For example, if your instructions stress the need to articulate, you will want to be certain that students have previously learned what this means. As an alternative, you might wish to include brief reminders in the instructions.

Most of these fluency activities do not include a formal assessment component. Should you wish to gauge a student's fluency improvement, we suggest that you track the student's progress at regular intervals using standardized assessment tools, such as running records (other alternatives are discussed in Chapter 7). Remember, providing students with fluency instruction, guidance, and practice should be a part of your larger literacy curriculum.

CHAPTER 7

Methods of Monitoring and Assessing Your Students' Literacy Bin Activities

There are numerous ways to keep track of your students' progress and performance with Literacy Bin Activities. In this chapter, we will provide a variety of methods to monitor and assess your students. In keeping with the flexible nature of the Literacy Bins and the activities, we don't prescribe one method of monitoring or assessing over another. Instead, we encourage you to pick and choose from those presented here or use others that might align with your district's standards or practices.

It is important, however, to keep in mind that the Literacy Bins are typically a component of a larger, integrated literacy approach. They are designed to supplement and enhance your reading instruction. As such, it may be necessary to consider how to coordinate your methods of monitoring and assessing. If you already rely on formal assessments in your reading instruction, you may choose a less formal method to evaluate your students' performance on their Literacy Bin Activities. You might also wish to supplement your instruction-based assessments with others used with the Literacy Bins, which could provide you with a more diverse understanding of your students' skills and abilities as well as their progress. Clearly, your decision on matters of monitoring and assessing will need some careful reflection.

Monitoring Techniques

Although the Literacy Bin Activities are to be completed independently by students, you will still want to observe and keep an eye on student performance and progress. Monitoring students is important so that you can provide helpful guidance and support as needed. In terms of student performance, you will want to be sure that students are participating in the activities as you had intended (i.e., within parameters to permit individual interpretation and varying levels of ability). If not, you may need to make adjustments by refining your activities or establishing better performance parameters for students to follow. In terms of student progress, you will want to reflect upon the following questions: Are students improving in building their background knowledge? Are they meeting higher levels of proficiency when applying the comprehension strategies? Is their fluency improving? Are they motivated by the activities? If your response to any of these questions is no, some adjustments may need to be made to the activity or to the manner in which a student engages with the activity. Ensuring that students gain the intended benefits of the literacy activities is the goal of monitoring.

Many teachers choose to monitor or review students' work after they have completed one or two activities. Others choose to monitor as students are in the process of working on an activity. This decision is best left to the teacher. Still, some degree of monitoring may be helpful, especially if students are typically working on Literacy Bin Activities unassisted by a teacher.

Quick Check

In order for many students to be successful with the type of independence allowed through Literacy Bin Activities, it is necessary that they first have a clear understanding of your expectations. As discussed in Chapter 2, creating guidelines for what constitutes "acceptable" work is a must that should be introduced with the first Literacy Bin batch of activities. Many of the teachers with whom we work rely on "a quick-check" system to establish guidelines. As shown in Figure 83, this phrase is an easy way for students to remember typical teacher expectations: "a" signifies "accurate," "quick" is for "quality work," and "check" means the work must be "complete." Therefore, when performing "a quick check" of a student's work, the teacher can look for these characteristics. Both the teacher and the student have the same understanding of what constitutes acceptable work.

Although many teachers adopt these expectations (or others like them), they typically involve their students in further shaping the expectations through group discussion. Building a classroom consensus on what each of

Figure 83. Sample Quick-Check Monitoring Form

A Quick-Check Form

Literacy Bin Activities

a = **a**ccurate _Be sure your content information is correct._

quick = **q**uality work _This work should be "best effort" quality._

check = **c**omplete _Be sure you completed all parts of the activity._

the three criteria means in student-friendly terms may encourage students to "buy in" and follow them. As shown in Figure 83, the students' ideas are recorded alongside each word. You may choose to create a classroom poster modeled after Figure 83, which will serve to remind students of the guidelines for acceptable work (see Appendix B for a reproducible version).

Despite taking every precaution that there is no misunderstanding, it may still be necessary to further clarify your expectations if you and a particular student do not share views; this is true even after you review the guidelines that the student helped to create. Demonstrating what you're looking for, either by showing other student work or by suggesting ways in which the student may improve his activity, may be helpful. Some teachers created sample activities and displayed them on an easel board near the Literacy Bins.

We have found that over time, most students develop a good understanding of what constitutes acceptable work. Still, it is important to remember that despite our good intentions to standardize our understanding of "best effort" and "quality," we must keep in mind the flexible nature of these terms. One student's best effort can result in a product that may look very different from another student's. Knowing your students' skills and abilities is vital. Also, it may take you some time to develop this understanding, especially as students engage in new and novel activities. The concept of best effort must be applied with a cautious regard for each student's unique skills and abilities.

Finding the time to monitor student activities is tricky, especially as most teachers choose to do this within the time allotted for their reading instruction. However, "a quick check" is just that; you spend very little time reviewing each student's work. Some ways to incorporate monitoring into your schedule are as follows:

- End your small-group instruction 3–5 minutes before the end of your reading period and call students who need "a quick check" to your reading table or desk where you can quickly review their completed activities.

- In the brief intervals between your reading groups, as students are coming and going, call those who are not gathering for their small-group instruction to meet you at your desk for "a quick check."

- Some teachers monitor student activities during brief periods of unscheduled time: the five minutes between lunch and recess, as students finish morning work and prior to the start of first period, as students return from lunch, or at dismissal time.

- Some teachers choose to monitor students' in-progress work in between their reading groups. Many have found this helpful for students who may need additional assistance. Although you will not be checking that the work is complete, you might wish to check on a student's accuracy and best effort.

- For Readers Theatre, other performance activities, and even some technology activities, you may need to schedule 10–15 minutes at the end of your reading time every other Friday, every Tuesday morning before announcements, or as needed to accommodate them. The reason for this is that some of the literacy activities ask students to perform in front of their "classroom audience." This is typically the case if students are developing skills through repeated practice. Ensuring that an audience is available to them is critical if students are to take seriously the importance of delivering quality work. Establishing a routine and encouraging students to sign up for performances will limit the need for extensive planning.

After checking a student's work, many teachers initial the student's tic-tac-toe game board in the space where the activity appears. This is an easy way to keep track of what's been checked and accepted.

Literacy Bin Observation

Another monitoring device is the "Literacy Bin Observation Form" shown in Figure 84 (see Appendix B for a reproducible version). This is used to collect data on observable behaviors that a student exhibits while working on the activities. As discussed earlier in the chapter, for the Literacy Bins to be a valuable component within your literacy instruction, students must be able to work on the activities independently. However, most students need to develop this independence; it is a skill that often needs nurturing. Specifically, some students may need assistance with the following:

- *Self-monitoring and managing their behavior*—Students may not have much experience working on their own and may therefore lack the ability to self-regulate their behavior. Reminding students of appropriate independent behaviors may be necessary.

- *Selecting activities*—Just as students often need assistance choosing books to read, so too may they need help selecting Literacy Bin Activities. Without proper guidance, students may hop from activity to activity and never complete any. Also, their inability to select an activity may prevent them from getting started. Helping students to identify activities they might like or encouraging them to try new activities might be necessary (see Figure 11 in Chapter 2 for suggestions).

Figure 84. Sample Literacy Bin Observation Form

Literacy Bin Observation of: _Samantha Liang_   **Date:** _March 12_
(Review tic-tac-toe game board and completed projects.)

- Demonstrates appropriate behavior: Yes ☑ No ☐
- Selects activities appropriately: Yes ☑ No ☐
- Uses appropriate pacing: Yes ☑ No ☐
- Works well in teams and independently: Yes ☑ No ☐
- Is self-sufficient: Yes ☑ No ☐

Comments: _Samantha has shown good improvement since the start of the school year. She has learned to work well independently, and she also takes her time to complete activities. Great job, Samantha!_

- *Appropriate pacing*—Typically, activities are not timed. However, it is still helpful to assist a student who may linger on one activity too long.

- *Working in teams*—In addition to working independently, students will also need to build team skills. Helping them resolve conflicts and communicate effectively with peers will enable them to be successful with many of the Literacy Bin Activities.

- *Self-sufficiency*—Resolving problems without the aid of a teacher is a skill that some students haven't developed. It may be necessary to provide them with helpful strategies if they can't find solutions to problems that stall their progress, such as unclear directions or inability to locate materials. "Ask three before me" is a well-known device where students ask three classmates for help prior to going to the teacher. Strategies like this may help as they build self-sufficiency.

In addition to noting these behaviors, you might also wish to provide comments to the following:

- Document a student's behavior
- Establish goals for your student
- Recognize improvements

You may wish to share the results of your observations with a student, especially if you're working toward strengthening a student's skill or modifying a challenging behavior (discussed later in this chapter). As such, the Literacy Bin Observation Form serves two purposes: It enables you to record student behavior, and it can help document plans and outcomes.

Determining how often to use a Literacy Bin Observation Form will vary from teacher to teacher. We have found that providing one or two observations per Literacy Bin per student will allow you to gather a good amount of information with which to note characteristics and, if need be, to monitor for growth and improvements.

Like "a quick-check" form of monitoring, the observation form can also be used during the following times:

- Just before the end of your literacy time (provided you end your guided reading instruction a few minutes early)
- In between your guided reading groups

- At other times when your students are able to work on their activities during those brief intervals of unscheduled times, such as before lunch and recess, and just after the morning work routine is completed

Need for Extensive Monitoring

As discussed in Chapter 1, Literacy Bin Activities can be used with all students. Likewise, the activities are primarily intended to be completed independently or in small collaborative groups. Still, some students may benefit from more extensive monitoring or additional support with some of the activities. Should this be the case, some ways to accommodate students' special needs are as follows:

- Provide "a quick check" after each activity or conduct frequent observations.
- Try to find an extra 3–5 minutes every other day to assist the student.
- Pair the student with a classmate.
- Involve other school professionals, such as resource professionals or literacy specialists, who may work with the student at various times throughout the day. Incorporate the Literacy Bin Activities in this instruction time with the student.
- Involve parents. In many cases, Literacy Bin Activities can be worked on at home. Explaining your objectives to parents for accurate, quality, and complete work will give them guidelines with which to help their child. Often, parents enjoy the novelty of the activities and are happy to help their children. Also, you may wish to send home your Literacy Bin Observation Forms for initialing or parent comments. Involve parents in helping to encourage positive change.

Some students may require this type of extra support throughout the school year, whereas others may only need some temporary assistance. Determining how to assist each student and how long to maintain the support is a decision best left to the teacher. You may wish to explore other ways to encourage and motivate students toward active participation in literacy-based activities (e.g., Athans & Devine, 2009).

Assessing Students' Activities

Although the intent of monitoring students' performance and progress is to ensure that everything is going according to plan, the intent of assessing students' performance and progress may be somewhat different. Monitoring often involves adjustments, such as those described earlier in this chapter, and thus may be viewed as a precursor stage to a formal assessment. On the other hand, an assessment suggests that a more formal evaluation is going to take place. Still, the distinction between monitoring and assessing and the ways in which both will be used with the Literacy Bin Activities are matters best left to the teacher, and districts often have their own views and guidelines about them.

Although a quick check and the Literacy Bin Observation Form are used for monitoring, they can also be used for assessing. For example, you could easily assign a numerical or alphabetic grade to a student's activity (or group of activities) based on the degree to which it was accurate, reflected quality work, and was complete. The same is true for each of the behaviors in the observation form. With your observations, you might also wish to provide an overall grade. Most teachers we worked with chose to consider these two tools as monitoring devices and use them to help students meet or exceed expectations. Many felt that the Literacy Bin Activities support a wide range of learning outcomes, making them difficult to assess with a standardized set of parameters. Still, this is a decision you can make based on your needs, district requirements, or other unique circumstances.

The Portfolio Checklist

The Portfolio Checklist is an assessment method used by many teachers who work with the Literacy Bins (see Figure 85 for an example; see Appendix B for a reproducible version). Here, students select one activity from those they completed from a themed Literacy Bin and include it in their Literacy Bin portfolio, which could be a plastic folder, large envelope, or other storage method. The Literacy Bin Portfolio Checklist is a device that many teachers use to help students make their selection. This checklist aligns with the quick-check monitoring tool, incorporating the expectations of accurate, quality, and complete work. It further encourages students to base their selection on other criteria as well, such as the uniqueness of the activity. Last, inviting students to explain why they chose their activity

Figure 85. Sample Literacy Bin Portfolio Checklist

Literacy Bin Portfolio Checklist for: <u>Michael Williams</u>

Bin: <u>Our Community</u>   **Date:** <u>November 5</u>

The work I've selected for my portfolio is:

- ☑ Accurate, quality work, complete!
- ☑ Represents my best efforts!
- ☑ Unique: there's no activity like it in my portfolio!
- ☑ Work that makes me proud!

I wanted to share this work because:

<u>I thought the word game was fun and a little harder than</u>
<u>ones in the first Literacy Bin we did. I had to take my time and</u>
<u>work really slow. Now I can say and spell every word, even the</u>
<u>really big ones!</u>

---

enables them to explore and then comment critically on other, more personal reflections of their work. Helping students learn to reflect upon and evaluate their own work is a positive side effect of using the checklist.

Teachers with whom we've worked have used anywhere from 4 to 15 themed Literacy Bins throughout the school year. Some ask students to select two activities from each Literacy Bin, whereas others don't impose a number limit and instead encourage students to use other criteria instead, such as the activity they enjoyed the most, a challenging activity, or an activity they never tried before. Should you choose to offer other options to students, you may wish to modify the checklist.

As some activities in the Literacy Bins may rely on the use of multimedia technologies, it may be necessary to store them electronically. For example, if students are creating slideshows, making digital movies, or working with other visual literacies, it may become necessary to store these activities on a flash drive, in a student's or teacher's technology file, or in a classroom file that can be shared. Similarly, you may wish to record students who are participating in any of the performing arts, including Readers Theatre activities, songs, and poetry readings, and store these electronically as well. Some teachers we worked with encouraged students to store multimedia activities in their technology files and also include some form of hard copy in their hard-copy portfolio, such as a photograph or a printed version of PowerPoint slides.

Many teachers designate time to invite students to share with classmates the activities they selected to include in their Literacy Bin portfolio. In these sharing sessions, students display their activities and give brief presentations about them, explaining why they selected them, discussing challenges they encountered, or describing techniques they used in the activities' construction. Incorporating the use and development of oral presentation and listening skills, such as those listed in Table 6, during students' sharing sessions is an excellent way to incorporate these important skills into your Literacy Bin Activities.

Table 6. Oral Presentation and Listening Skills

Process of Presenting	Oral and Speaking Skills	Use of Support Devices and Props	Listening Skills	Skills for Providing Feedback
Student demonstrates an understanding that the presentation should: • Flow smoothly from start to finish • Be well organized • Make good use of appropriate materials and technology • Reflect the student's concern for accuracy and best effort • Demonstrate an awareness of the audience	Student demonstrates skill using: • Appropriate voice (i.e., intonation) • Appropriate fluency and pace • Appropriate expression	Student demonstrates skill using: • Props that enhance the presentation • Other devices that enhance the presentation	As an audience member, student demonstrates: • Active listening skills (i.e., eyes focused on the speaker, attentiveness, and responsiveness) • Respectful viewing behaviors (i.e., quiet, courteous, and considerate of performers) • An ability to acquire information through note taking or other means	Student demonstrates skill: • Discussing strengths of a presentation • Expressing opinions • Supporting opinions with details • Recognizing an awareness of others' feelings

Targeted Assessment Rubrics

As described in Chapter 1, teachers may suggest that certain students complete assigned activities before selecting ones on their own. This is done to help students strengthen targeted skills, based on a need the teacher identified during small-group instruction. Should this be the case, teachers may wish to incorporate a more formal assessment of a student's performance with these activities, so they have documentation that could be used to help initiate further support for the student. Using one of the monitoring methods discussed earlier for assessment purposes is one way to go about this. Another way is to use a rubric.

Should you wish to formally assess a student's activities or overall performance using the Literacy Bins, you may wish to create generic rubrics that address each of the objectives of the Literacy Bin Activities, such as improving fluency, building background knowledge, and practicing comprehension strategies, and the degree of participation in the activities (to demonstrate motivation). Examples of each type of rubric are featured in Figure 86 (see Appendix B for reproducible versions). Determining key elements of the tasks will guide you as you evaluate each student's performance. You might wish to create broad key elements so that they will apply to all of the same type of literacy activities within a Literacy Bin. For example, the Comprehension Practice Rubric can be used for all comprehension activities despite differing strategies. Similarly, the Fluency Rubric can be used for all fluency activities, although they will differ. Determining what your key elements will be and how many there should be is a decision best left to the teacher.

As many of the activities include a writing component, you may wish to assess this separately, such as by using the second set of the rubrics featured in Figure 86. This set can be copied onto the reverse side of the first set. For example, the Comprehension Practice and the Background Knowledge rubrics featured in the examples make use of the writing rubric. Using the writing rubric in this manner is also a decision best left to the teacher. It is important to identify key elements of the task, so students are aware of the criteria used for their assessment.

Another variation on the use of rubrics is a double-rubric system. Here, students are asked to evaluate their performance. After reviewing the student's self-evaluation, the teacher may agree or disagree with the student. Should there be disagreement, the teacher will mark the rubric,

Figure 86. Sample Literacy Bin Activity Assessment Rubrics

Comprehension Practice Rubric

Name: _Bethany G._   Date: _Oct. 18_

Literacy Bin Theme: _Colonial Times_

Activity #: _6_

Demonstration of key elements of task:

Strategy is used correctly.   4 (3) 2 1

Strategy is used consistently.   4 (3) 2 1

Examples show in-depth grasp.   4 (3) 2 1

_____   4 3 2 1

Participation: _Bethany tackled her summarizing activity enthusiastically. She located materials quickly and set to work summarizing events from the reading passage._

Effort: _Bethany remained focused and attentive as she worked on her summarizing activity. Her effort was also evident in the written component of the task where she recorded her summary (see reverse)._

4 = accomplished; 3 = proficient; 2 = progressing with difficulty; 1 = not progressing

Vocabulary Knowledge & Word Skills Rubric

Name: _Sean W._   Date: _Oct. 18_

Literacy Bin Theme: _Colonial Times_

Activity #: _1_

Demonstration of key elements of task:

Word work is accurate.   (4) 3 2 1

Word work is consistent.   (4) 3 2 1

Word knowledge is evident.   (4) 3 2 1

Demonstration is strong.   (4) 3 2 1

Participation: _Sean worked well with his team to portray the vocabulary words in this unit. Each member of the team contributed to the activities effectively._

Effort: _Sean put forth excellent effort and extended the word activities by researching the history of the words on his own. The class thoroughly enjoyed his information and gained valuable new knowledge because of his extra effort._

4 = accomplished; 3 = proficient; 2 = progressing with difficulty; 1 = not progressing

Background Knowledge Rubric

Name: _Sarah S._   Date: _Oct. 18_

Literacy Bin Theme: _Colonial Times_

Activity #: _9_

Demonstration of key elements of task:

Information is accurate.   4 (3) 2 1

Information is thorough.   4 (3) 2 1

Depth of knowledge is evident.   4 3 (2) 1

_____   4 3 2 1

Participation: _Sarah eagerly captured the essence of colonial times in her comic book rendition of "A Day in the Life of a Colonial Family."_

Effort: _Sarah used good effort selecting activities for her comic book, and her illustrations were good. Some minor trouble with content writing & spelling (see reverse)._

4 = accomplished; 3 = proficient; 2 = progressing with difficulty; 1 = not progressing

Fluency Rubric

Name: _Tyrell C._   Date: _Oct. 18_

Literacy Bin Theme: _Colonial Times_

Activity #: _8_

Demonstration of key elements of task:

Skills are applied accurately.   4 3 (2) 1

Skills are applied consistently.   4 3 (2) 1

Skills show in-depth grasp.   4 3 (2) 1

Demonstration is strong.   4 (3) 2 1

Participation: _Tyrell has made some improvement working with teammates, although he sometimes benefits from reminders to stay focused on competing his work._

Effort: _Tyrell is beginning to use improved effort, and I want to encourage him to continue monitoring this in all of his literacy activities._

4 = accomplished; 3 = proficient; 2 = progressing with difficulty; 1 = not progressing

(continued)

Figure 86. Sample Literacy Bin Activity Assessment Rubrics (*continued*)

Comprehension Practice Rubric: Writing

Name: _Bethany G._   Date: _Oct. 18_

Literacy Bin Theme: _Colonial Times_

Activity #: _6_

Addresses the topic: Main idea is present, task answered, understands topic, and provides relevant written response.   4 ③ 2 1

Details: Develops ideas with support using examples, connections, further description, etc.   4 ③ 2 1

Organization: Has a logical and orderly plan, strong transitions, and correct paragraphing.   4 ③ 2 1

Mechanics: Uses correct capitalization, punctuation, spelling, and grammar, and handwriting is legible with letters and words formed and spaced correctly.   4 ③ 2 1

Effort: _Bethany's summary was well written and concise. Her attention to selecting main ideas was evident and her writing skills were very good._

4 = accomplished; 3 = proficient; 2 = progressing with difficulty; 1 = not progressing

---

Vocabulary Knowledge & Word Skills Rubric: Writing

Name: _____   Date: _____

Literacy Bin Theme: _____

Activity #: _____

Addresses the topic: Main idea is present, task answered, understands topic, and provides relevant written response.   4 3 2 1

Details: Develops ideas with support using examples, connections, further description, etc.   4 3 2 1

Organization: Has a logical and orderly plan, strong transitions, and correct paragraphing.   4 3 2 1

Mechanics: Uses correct capitalization, punctuation, spelling, and grammar, and handwriting is legible with letters and words formed and spaced correctly.   4 3 2 1

Effort: _____

4 = accomplished; 3 = proficient; 2 = progressing with difficulty; 1 = not progressing

---

Background Knowledge Rubric: Writing

Name: _Sarah S._   Date: _Oct. 18_

Literacy Bin Theme: _Colonial Times_

Activity #: _9_

Addresses the topic: Main idea is present, task answered, understands topic, and provides relevant written response.   4 ③ 2 1

Details: Develops ideas with support using examples, connections, further description, etc.   4 3 ② 1

Organization: Has a logical and orderly plan, strong transitions, and correct paragraphing.   4 ③ 2 1

Mechanics: Uses correct capitalization, punctuation, spelling, and grammar, and handwriting is legible with letters and words formed and spaced correctly.   4 3 ② 1

Effort: _Sarah had trouble with spelling and grasping the roles of family members. We discussed how she could use more effort while reading the passage in the Bin._

4 = accomplished; 3 = proficient; 2 = progressing with difficulty; 1 = not progressing

---

Fluency Rubric: Writing

Name: _____   Date: _____

Literacy Bin Theme: _____

Activity #: _____

Addresses the topic: Main idea is present, task answered, understands topic, and provides relevant written response.   4 3 2 1

Details: Develops ideas with support using examples, connections, further description, etc.   4 3 2 1

Organization: Has a logical and orderly plan, strong transitions, and correct paragraphing.   4 3 2 1

Mechanics: Uses correct capitalization, punctuation, spelling, and grammar, and handwriting is legible with letters and words formed and spaced correctly.   4 3 2 1

Effort: _____

4 = accomplished; 3 = proficient; 2 = progressing with difficulty; 1 = not progressing

then meet with the student to discuss and plan ways to remedy the difference of opinions. If there is agreement, the teacher may return the rubric with a comment acknowledging agreement with the student. Several teachers we've worked with place a "great minds think alike" stamp on the students' rubrics and return them for the students to see.

Monitoring and Assessing Your Literacy Bin Activities Using Students' Views

The tools used to monitor and assess your students' participation with the Literacy Bins will provide you with insightful information with which to supplement your knowledge about your students' literacy skills and abilities. Likewise, these same tools will allow you to determine the effectiveness of the activities in your Literacy Bins. As you perform a quick check on your students' activities and conduct student observations, you can draw many conclusions about the activities or processes you used. These conclusions can help to improve your current as well as your future Literacy Bins. Ensuring that the Literacy Bin Activities are truly meeting your instructional objectives is something you will always want to keep in check, and the feedback you get from your students can help steer you toward success and continual improvement. As an example, observing your students as they engage in the activities will help you answer the following questions:

- Were directions clear?
- Were materials suitable?
- Did your objectives align with the outcomes for all activities?
- Did the activities take an appropriate amount of time?
- Were students as successful as you had intended?
- Was the difficulty level of the activities varied and appropriate?
- Was the blend of independent and team activities appropriate?
- Were students successful incorporating the use of technology into their activities?

In addition to gaining useful information from the monitoring and assessment tools, you might also wish to use a student survey to learn your students' thoughts and ideas, which they might not otherwise have the chance to express. Figure 87 is a sample of an "A Penny for Your Thoughts" Survey (see Appendix B for a reproducible version). Teachers who use this survey often give students a candy coin or a piece of penny candy to enjoy while they complete it. Through the use of a survey, you may be able to improve the quality of your Literacy Bins by creating new activities, reshaping others, or eliminating and replacing ones that don't

Figure 87. Sample "A Penny for Your Thoughts" Survey

Name: _Erica Jenison_   Date: _March 12_

"A Penny for Your Thoughts" on the
_____The Revolutionary Period & the New Nation_____ Literacy Bin!

• How many activities were you able to complete? __7__

• How would you rate the quality of your work? Place an X on the scale.

4	3	2	1

• Did you understand the directions for all of the activities? Were any tricky?
I understood all the directions, but I had to read part of the ones for Activity 8 about the Constitution carefully. Jen read them aloud with me, and then we figured out what we were supposed to do right away. It turned out to be fun.

• Were you able to complete the activities on your own or with a little help from classmates? Please explain.
I did a lot of activities on my own and a few with Phillip, Amy, and Tyrell. Phillip and I wrote a Revolutionary rap together. Tyrell asked Amy and me to do Genius TV Talk Show with him. He helped me with some of the big vocabulary words.

• Do you feel the activities in this Literacy Bin helped you? If so, how?
I think the activities helped, because I learned things about the Constitution I didn't know from social studies class. I also feel good about the new vocabulary words I'm learning. I understand what I'm reading, even the harder words.

• What kinds of activities would you like us to include in the next Literacy Bin?
I really liked working with the website and want more activities where I can use the computer. I also liked taking books home to read. Maybe we could write our own books at home, too, and bring them in to show our friends. That would be fun.

work, based on comments provided by your students. Involving students in the design and development of your Literacy Bins is one of the best ways to ensure the success of the activities. Some teachers have students take a survey at the end of each Literacy Bin or after every other one, which is a decision best left to each teacher.

MOVING FORWARD

As discussed in this chapter, there are numerous ways to keep score of your students' progress as they work with the Literacy Bin Activities. You can use the monitoring and assessing devices to ensure that students are meeting your expectations for quality and effort, progressing in their ability to learn independently, and that they are gaining valuable literacy skills that supplement your reading instruction. Yet another outcome you will want to watch for are ways in which students demonstrate their new knowledge or skills aside from the avenues that are directly linked to the Literacy Bins. For example, ask yourself the following:

- Are students discussing new ideas they've learned while in their small-group instruction?
- Are they using vocabulary words in their writing journals that were introduced in a Literacy Bin Activity?
- Is their reading fluency improving as you informally listen to students read during group instruction (and when you conduct a formal running record)?
- Are students excited about the activities and talking about them as they plan their big performance?
- Are you able to witness new interests emerging from students who previously seemed disinterested?
- Are students working with peers they typically didn't work with before?
- Are clusters of students sharing their excitement about their newly found common interests?

Finding evidence of these types of activities lets you know the score is in your favor.

CHAPTER 8

Literacy Bin Activities: Frequently Asked Questions

Question: How often should I change my Literacy Bin Activities?

Answer: The Literacy Bin Activities should be kept in place long enough for the students to have time to complete a selection of activities. Typically we have changed our Literacy Bins every 6–8 weeks. This usually covers 1–2 units and allows students ample time to practice and complete a sufficient number of activities.

Question: Do all of the Literacy Bin Activities need to be on the same topic?

Answer: As we strongly support the use of Literacy Bins to supplement instruction, most of our Literacy Bin Activities are related to the topics or units we are studying. We have seen many examples of activities combining other subjects or topics. We have even seen monthly bins that included activities from all subjects and themes being covered that month. In all cases, the activities should reinforce and support class instruction.

Question: Can I reuse Literacy Bin Activities?

Answer: Yes, you can repeat games and activities that have been exceptionally popular or successful. You may also modify an activity to match the current theme or content; for example, creating a commercial or comic strip can be modified to enhance a variety of units of study. Oftentimes, repeating an activity helps the students feel more confident and creative when completing a task.

Question: Are students able to complete the activities independently?

Answer: Once introduced with minimal directions from the teacher, the activities are usually self-directed. Some can be completed with a partner or group, which will aid students who may have difficulty with directions.

Question: Where can I get ideas and materials for my Literacy Bins?

Answer: There are endless possible resources for Literacy Bin ideas and materials. Many teacher magazines offer helpful tips, lesson ideas, and activities that relate to specific content or subjects. Websites and supplemental reading materials are readily available in most schools. It is also helpful to share materials and ideas with other teachers.

Question: What tips should I keep in mind as I create my own activities?

Answer: Don't hesitate to explore novel and creative ways to address your objectives. Some of our quirky, imaginative ideas have produced excellent results, based on student participation and evidence of skill development. Designing activities around zany game shows, outlandish talent competitions, and even academic-based sporting events are usually big hits. Still, some of the simple activities we include continue to be favorites as well. Over time, you'll develop a sense of what types of activities will work and what will flop. The same is true with your skill at creating successful, engaging activities. Getting the knack of making activities will come.

Question: How much time is needed to complete the Literacy Bin Activities?

Answer: The amount of time needed will vary. Some activities, such as drama or Readers Theatre, will take preparation and practice, whereas a vocabulary game may require only a few minutes to complete. Creating a book or comic strip can take more or less time, depending on the directions and effort. We try to create a mix of activities that students can finish fairly quickly and others that are more involved.

Question: Do the students need to work on the activities every day?

Answer: The Literacy Bin Activities are designed to support and supplement your guided reading instruction. Students may work with the Literacy Bins when they are not in their guided reading groups or whenever they have free time. The teacher may set aside extra time for the class to work on activities, and some can be completed at home.

Question: What if some students are unable to complete the activities?

Answer: Some students easily work through many activities, whereas others have difficulty completing enough of them to make a three-in-a-row tic-tac-toe. Providing some activities that can be completed in class and others that can be completed at home may help some students finish one or more tic-tac-toes. Letting the students work with a partner or group and providing activities that appeal to a variety of learning styles and modalities will provide ample opportunity for all students to be successful.

Question: How do I grade my Literacy Bin Activities?

Answer: Some teachers simply offer credit for how many tic-tac-toes each student completes or counts each box for points. Others do not associate a grade or points but allow students to earn trinkets or stickers for completing the activities. Some teachers use a simple rubric to score completed activities. One benefit of Literacy Bin Activities is their flexibility; they can be scored in whatever way serves the needs of the classroom. Chapter 7 provides more information on tools and methods for grading Literacy Bin Activities.

Question: Can I incorporate some required work in my Literacy Bins?

Answer: Yes, we have worked with teachers who have incorporated a variety of other activities into the Literacy Bins. For example, teachers often include word work and other types of activities that are components of their district initiatives. The flexible nature of the Literacy Bins can easily accommodate this.

Question: How can I improve my activities?

Answer: Once you get started, be prepared to evaluate the effectiveness of your activities by observing your students and collecting data. Ways in which you can collect information are presented in Chapter 7. Still, you will want to launch your Literacy Bins with this in mind, so to glean useful information as it unfolds, ask yourself questions such as, Which activities attracted students? Could an activity be changed to better reflect its intended objective? Did an activity require too much time? Were the instructions clear? and Was there evidence that student skill was improved? Knowing answers to these types of questions will help you shape future Literacy Bin Activities.

Reproducible Game Boards and Sample Directions

The material in Appendix A includes a variety of sample tic-tac-toe game boards. You can use these as they are, adapt them to your needs and grade level, or use them as models to create your own boards. Sample directions for literacy activities have also been included.

- Blank Tic-Tac-Toe Game Board
- Tic-Tac-Toe Game Board for Tall Tales Unit
- Tic-Tac-Toe Game Board for Native Americans Unit
- Tic-Tac-Toe Game Board for Colonial Times Unit
- Tic-Tac-Toe Game Board for Revolutionary Period and the New Nation Unit
- Tic-Tac-Toe Game Board for Immigration and the Erie Canal Unit
- Tic-Tac-Toe Game Board for U.S. Presidents Unit
- Tic-Tac-Toe Game Board for Community Unit
- Tic-Tac-Toe Game Board for Plants Unit
- Tic-Tac-Toe Game Board for Earth's Surface Unit
- Tic-Tac-Toe Game Board for Literacy
- Tic-Tac-Toe Game Board for Spelling
- Directions for Colonial Times Word Activities
- Directions for Immigration Background Knowledge Glyph
- Directions for Writing RAFTs for Grades 1, 3, 4, and 6

Name: _____

Name: _____

Tall Tales

Tic-Tac-Toe

Word Search
Tall Tales

Find and highlight all of the words from the word bank. Get ready to s-t-r-e-t-c-h your imagination!

(There's an extra-credit crossword puzzle, too!)

Figurative Language

Can you find some creative and colorful similes, metaphors, idioms, and personification in the pocket of tall tales?

Batter Up!

"Casey at the Bat" is an American tall tale about a famous baseball player. Here, the story is presented as a *choral reading*. This means you find a buddy or two and read it aloud. Practice, practice, practice, then record your reading!

COMIC BOOK WRITERS WANTED!

Create and illustrate a mini comic book about your favorite tall tale character and his or her dashing escapades.

READ
Read at Home!

Have your parent sign your reading list of a minimum of five tall tales. Bonus points will be awarded for special research challenge.

TRUTH OR EXAGGERATION?
YOU BE THE JUDGE...

Use a T-chart to list as many truths and exaggerations as you can find in the sample story.

Drama!
(library pass needed)

Try out some of these tall tale Readers Theatre plays. You can find some friends to read with you. Practice, practice, practice, and perhaps you'll get a chance to perform!

Dare to Compare!

Compare and contrast two tall tales using a Venn diagram.

Author for Hire!

Write your own tall tale! Be the main character or make up one. A prewriting graphic organizer will help guide you. **Be creative!**

Fun-tastic Activities for Differentiating Comprehension Instruction, Grades 2–6 by Sandra K. Athans and Denise Ashe Devine. © 2010 by the International Reading Association.

127

Native Americans

Tic-Tac-Toe

Word Search
Native Americans

Find and highlight all of the words from the word bank. Get ready to enter a new world!

What's the Big Idea?

Can you find the main or big ideas about a Native American hero? Make a large, colorful poster to honor your hero and nominate them to appear on a postage stamp!

Poetry Buddy

Hiawatha was a legendary Native American leader. Here, the story of his boyhood is presented in a poem. Find a buddy or two and listen to the cassette while following in the book. Then, practice reading it aloud!

COMIC BOOK WRITERS WANTED!

Create and illustrate a mini comic book, retelling your favorite Native American pourquoi story or legend.

READ
Read at Home!

Have your parent sign your reading list of a minimum of five books on Native Americans. These are on reserve in the library for overnight borrowing.

Are You Smarter Than a Fourth Grader?

Read the sheets to find some good facts and details that you can turn into questions. Get ready to stump your parents and friends.

Drama!
(library pass needed)

Try out either of these Native American Readers Theatre plays. You can find some friends to read with you. Practice, practice, practice, and perhaps you'll get a chance to perform!

What's for Dinner?

If you were to plan a Native American meal, what would it include and why?

A Day in the Life
of a Native American Child

Pretend you are a Native American boy or girl and write a diary entry about a day in your life. Illustrate your diary, too!

Fun-tastic Activities for Differentiating Comprehension Instruction, Grades 2–6 by Sandra K. Athans and Denise Ashe Devine. © 2010 by the International Reading Association.

Colonial Times

Vocabulary Activity

Select one of the three word games from the sheet in the Literacy Bin:

1. Picture This
2. Poetry Vocabulary
3. Slap, Tap, & Snap

Use the words from the "Colonial Times Vocabulary List" on that sheet to complete your activity.

IT HAPPENED WHEN?

TIMELINE ACTIVITY

Can you organize these important events into the correct chronological order? Use the dates as your guide. Look at the sequence of events that unfolds.

Genius TV Talk Show!

A scholarly showing of smarts
(library pass needed for filming)

Our extremely intelligent student scholars will share their smarts about common questions on the Colonial period—live—on the popular talk show "Genius TV Talk Show." They've got smarts, they've got style...and just listen to them speak!

Colonial Leaders Hall of Fame!

Create a portrait of a leader to hang in the Colonial Hall of Fame and include a paragraph about your leader's accomplishments.
Select from: Henry Hudson, Peter Minuit, Peter Stuyvesant, John Peter Zenger, Elias Neau, Samuel Fraunces, General George Washington, Joseph Brant, Sagoyewatha, or George Clinton.

READ

Read at Home!

Have your parent sign your reading list of a minimum of five Colonial nonfiction books. *My Prairie Year* and *Sarah, Plain and Tall* are works of historical fiction. You can swap either of these in place of *two* nonfiction titles.

WHAT HAPPENED... AND WHY?

CAUSE & EFFECT!

Use a cause-and-effect chart and find at least five examples in the book *New York as a Dutch Colony* and then five other examples in the book *New York as an English Colony*.

Drama!

You will perform a one-person character play. Grab the spotlight and a book (Sarah Morton or Samuel Eaton) and tell your story (read it aloud) as if you were a pilgrim child growing up in 1627. Practice, practice, practice, and perhaps you'll get a chance to record your play!

Dare to Compare!

Compare and contrast Colonial school days to today's school days. Read the article "Colonial Schools" and the book *Colonial Teachers* to help.

Colonial Sites

Visit some Colonial websites where you can learn more about this fascinating time in our history. Record five new facts you've learned, and let us know if you'd recommend this site to your classmates!

Fun-tastic Activities for Differentiating Comprehension Instruction, Grades 2–6 by Sandra K. Athans and Denise Ashe Devine. © 2010 by the International Reading Association.

Name: _____

The Revolutionary Period & the New Nation Tic-Tac-Toe

Word Search **The Revolutionary Period** Find and highlight all of the words from the word bank. *Hurry! The British are coming!*	**What Are You Inferring?** Write some insightful captions and speech bubbles for these historical pictures and cartoons!	**NO TAXATION WITHOUT REPRESENTATION!** We're looking for a new American Revolutionary Idol! Write a song or rap about this catchy phrase and perform in the competition!
COMIC BOOK WRITERS WANTED! Create and illustrate a mini comic book about your favorite event or battle from the Revolutionary War. Find a book in the bin for ideas. You may also choose an event during the formation of our New Nation.	**READ** **Read at Home!** Have your parent sign your reading list of a minimum of five Revolutionary War or government titles. *Buttons for General Washington* or *Secret Soldier* can be swapped for two books.	**Are You Smarter Than a Fourth Grader?** Read the book *Governing New York* and find some good facts and details that you can turn into questions. Get ready to stump your parents and friends.
Drama! (library pass needed) Try out these Readers Theatre scripts, "**The Constitution of the United States**" or "**Patriots and Loyalists**," or **Genius TV Talk Show**, back by popular demand. Hear our genius students share their knowledge on the Constitution!	**Buddy Up & Create a Classroom Constitution** What freedoms and rules do you think should be followed in our classroom? Pattern your constitution after America's. Be creative!	**Revolutionary Period & Government Websites** Visit some Revolutionary War and government websites to learn more about these interesting times in our history. Record five facts you've learned and let us know if you'd recommend this site to others.

Fun-tastic Activities for Differentiating Comprehension Instruction, Grades 2–6 by Sandra K. Athans and Denise Ashe Devine. © 2010 by the International Reading Association.

Immigration & the Erie Canal

Tic-Tac-Toe

Word Searches
Immigration & the Erie Canal

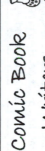

Find and highlight all of the words from the word bank. Hurry, get ready to travel to new places and board new vessels!

What's the Big Idea?!

Using a copy of *Kids Discover: Immigration*, select any three of these main articles:

"A Nation of Immigrants," "The Immigrant Experience," "A New Wave," "It's the Law" and identify the big idea in each article.

A Day in the Life of an Immigrant Child

Pretend you are an immigrant boy or girl and write a one-page (or more) diary entry about a day in your life. Read the diary aloud to another class.

Comic Book Writers Wanted!

Create and illustrate a mini comic book about life on the Erie Canal. Be sure to include content vocabulary and illustrations.

Read at Home or to Third Graders at Recess!

Have your parent sign your reading list of a minimum of five books on immigration and the Erie Canal. Choose from a selection on reserve at the library.

LOW BRIDGE! EVERYBODY DOWN!
Musicians & Song Writers Wanted!

Write a new verse for this popular canal song and perform it with your friends!

Drama!
(library pass needed)

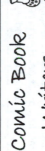

Try out some of these Erie Canal Readers Theatre plays. You can find some friends who would like to read with you. Practice, practice, practice, and perhaps you'll get a chance to perform!

The Art of Sequencing...
A Picture Game!

On index cards, illustrate and provide captions for 7–10 events that many immigrants experienced as they passed through Ellis Island. Have a classmate try to put them in the correct sequence.

WEBSITES & VIRTUAL TOURS

Visit some of the immigration and Erie Canal websites in your Favorites folder. List at least five new facts you learn about each. Let us know if you'd recommend this site to others.

Fun-tastic Activities for Differentiating Comprehension Instruction, Grades 2–6 by Sandra K. Athans and Denise Ashe Devine. © 2010 by the International Reading Association.

131

Vocabulary Activity

Select one of these three word games from the sheet in the Literacy Bin:

1. Create a Stamp
2. Poetry Vocabulary
3. Casting Call

Use the words from the "Presidential Vocabulary List" on that sheet to complete your activity.

U.S. Presidents Trading Cards

Design and create a set of information-packed trading cards for at least five former presidents. On one side of the card, you should create an illustration. On the other side, include important details and interesting facts.

What a Great Imposter!

Practice a brief speech pretending that you are a former U.S. President. Choose a book about him from the Literacy Bin Library. You may create props or scenery to help you to be *a great imposter!*

Row, Row, Row Your Boat
Row, Row, Row Your Boat
Row, Row, Row Your Boat

Choose a president's biography from the Literacy Bin Library. Find two friends and write a song about this president's life. Be sure to include important information and details about his life. Practice, practice, practice, then perform your song in a round.

READ
Read at Home!

Have your parent sign your reading list of a minimum of five presidential biographies.

Bonus: Create a portrait and brief summary on one president you read about.

Did You Know...?

Work with a partner or by yourself to search several U.S. presidents' websites for 10 (or more) interesting or unusual facts to share with the class.

Presidential Facts

1. Can you match the presidents' photos with the correct names?
2. Can you match each president with his vice president?
3. Can you put the presidents in the correct sequential order starting with George Washington?

Use the books from the Literacy Bin Library to check your answers.

Dare to Compare!

Compare and contrast two U.S. presidents using a Venn diagram.

"May I Quote You?"

Read each of these quotes from a former U.S. president and rewrite them in your own words.

Fun-tastic Activities for Differentiating Comprehension Instruction, Grades 2–6 by Sandra K. Athans and Denise Ashe Devine. © 2010 by the International Reading Association.

Name: _____

Community

Meet "S-t-r-e-t-c-h"

My friend Mr. Stretch likes to s-t-r-e-t-c-h every sound in every word. Pretend you're Stretch and practice reading the "Community Word List" by stretching out each sound. Share your stretched-out performance with your classmates.

Looking for Skilled Puppeteers!

Create a skit about a job or event in our community using puppets. You may make a puppet using the art materials in the basket labeled #2. Practice your puppet show, then share with an audience.

PUZZLED

WHAT'S THE BIG PICTURE?

Read the clues on the back of each puzzle piece to make a picture of something in our community.

Go to the Head of the Classroom...

Pretend you are the teacher. You must teach your class how to use "fix-up" strategies when they don't understand the passages on community helpers.

READ

Read at Home!

Sign out three "community" books to read at home with your family. Have an adult sign your sheet and bring it back to school.

Word Gallery Showcase

featuring

Vocabulary to Show Off

Choose five vocabulary words to display in a fancy, colorful, and interesting way! Be sure to spell every word carefully and make each letter "picture perfect." Place your favorites in the vocabulary showcase!

Rah! Rah! Rah!

Let's give a cheer for the people in our community! Choose a book about community helpers from the Literacy Bin Library and create a cheer about their job. Practice your cheer and share it with the class...cheerfully!

Connection Caboodle

Play with a partner. Each partner picks one "job" card and shares a connection: Text-to-Text Text-to-Self Text-to-World

Challenge: Can you make all three types of connections with one card?

Fact or Fiction?

Sort the "fact or fiction?" cards into two groups: true and false. Use the books from the Literacy Bin to check any that you are unsure of.

Bonus: Use the books to find information to create your own "fact or fiction?" cards to add to our game.

Fun-tastic Activities for Differentiating Comprehension Instruction, Grades 2–6 by Sandra K. Athans and Denise Ashe Devine. © 2010 by the International Reading Association.

133

Name: _____

Plants

Fancy Word Close-Ups!

Using the vocabulary list provided in the Literacy Bin, rewrite each word fancifully and display it in our Greenhouse Museum. Be careful with spelling, because some of the words are tricky!

Photosynthesis Teaching Book

Use the large paper in the art basket to create a teaching book to share with the class. Be sure to include detailed information and illustrations.

Alien Tour Guide

Congratulations! You and a buddy have been selected to be tour guides for a group of alien students who will be visiting our town. They are most interested in our plant life, because they have no plants on their planet. Create a PowerPoint presentation for the aliens to take back to their planet, explaining the parts of a plant, how plants reproduce, what plants need to survive, and different types of plants. Have fun!

Plant Poetry

Using books from the Literacy Bin Library and words from the plant vocabulary list, create a poem about plants. Practice reading your poem, then share it with the class.

READ Read at Home!

Have your parent sign your reading list of a minimum of five plant-related articles after you've read them.

"JEOPARDY"

Work with a group of two to four students to create a "Jeopardy" game for the class. Read several of the books or articles from the basket and create leveled questions. Be prepared to quiz your classmates.

What's My Job?

Match each part of the plant with its job. Use the books in the Literacy Bin Library to check your work.

Word-Game-Master

Create your own game using words from the plant vocabulary list. Be sure your game helps others learn the meaning of the words or helps others build their skills working with words.

The Master

The Great Seed Mystery

Someone mixed up Farmer Brown's seeds! How will he know if he has planted pumpkins or lima beans? Use our plant books, plant websites, and what you have learned about seeds to help Farmer Brown identify what types of seeds he has.

Fun-tastic Activities for Differentiating Comprehension Instruction, Grades 2–6 by Sandra K. Athans and Denise Ashe Devine. © 2010 by the International Reading Association.

Name: _____

Earth's Surface

SEISMOGRAPH

Use the letters from the word *SEISMOGRAPH* to make as many words as you can. Make sure you write them all down!

Which food looks closest to the Earth's layers and why?

orange, avocado, or pear

Math Challenge

See if you can find the answer to this math challenge.

Caption Match

Follow the directions on the caption match paper. Check your answers with a friend when you are finished.

The Earth's Layers

Use the direction sheet to guide you in making a model of the Earth's layers. This will be a great study tool!

Brain Pop

Watch the earthquake Brain Pop video on the computer **twice**. When you finish, take the online quiz to see what you remember!

Pair~Share Reading

Read the short story about volcanoes with a partner.

Song or Poem

Write a catchy song or poem about an earthquake that is at least four lines long.

Writing Prompt

What would you do to prepare for an earthquake? Write at least one paragraph using complete sentences.

Note. Adapted from a game board created by Danielle Bosco and Jaclyn Hanifin from the Baldwinsville Central School District, New York. Reprinted with permission.

Fun-tastic Activities for Differentiating Comprehension Instruction, Grades 2–6 by Sandra K. Athans and Denise Ashe Devine. © 2010 by the International Reading Association.

Literacy · Tic-Tac-Toe

Think-Alongs

Use think-alongs to assist in your comprehension of the book you are reading.

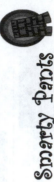

Mad Libs

Use mad libs to broaden your vocabulary. Make a really funny story by changing the nouns in a picture book.

Be Elaborate!

This assignment is as cool as your favorite team winning the championship in six overtimes! Use this station to practice elaboration in your writing.

Scoop and Spell

Practice your spelling by randomly choosing a letter and writing down as many words as you can think of that start with that letter.

Is That a Fact?

Test how much you know! Write down 10 facts you can recall from our latest unit, then check your book to see if you were right.

Smarty Pants

Explore the picture books in the front of the room, then fill out a smart chart for each book you read.

Nouns and Verbs

This will help you "breathe life" into your writing!

Use the dictionary or thesaurus to swap out nouns and verbs in a picture book.

Knowledge Check!

This will be a time-consuming challenge for you and a partner!

Read two online newspaper articles and search online for the definitions of any words you don't recognize.

Internal Character Setups

Read a picture book, then fill in a T-chart for the book.

Note. Adapted from a game board created by Christie Brooks from the Baldwinsville Central School District, New York. Reprinted with permission.

Fun-tastic Activities for Differentiating Comprehension Instruction, Grades 2–6 by Sandra K. Athans and Denise Ashe Devine. © 2010 by the International Reading Association.

Name: _____

Spelling

Bingo!	Stamps	White Writing
With two to four partners, have each person secretly write a different spelling list word in each square on a bingo sheet. Then, pull words out of a hat one at a time to play!	Stamp out each letter of your spelling words.	Take black paper and write your words two times in white pencil. 
Stencils	Sentences	Magnet Letters
Take a set of stencils and trace each letter of your words.	Pick the four words that are most difficult for you to spell, then write a sentence for each word.	Use magnets to form your spelling words.
Glitter Glue	FOAM LETTERS	Rice
Write each word on paper with a tube of glitter glue. **Variation:** Write each word in a different color.	Form each of your spelling words with a set of foam letters.	Take a cup of rice and a plastic dish. Write each of your spelling words in the rice.

Note. Adapted from a game board created by Diane FitzGibbons, Debbie Genalo, and Mary Wisniewski from the Baldwinsville Central School District, New York. Reprinted with permission.

Fun-tastic Activities for Differentiating Comprehension Instruction, Grades 2–6 by Sandra K. Athans and Denise Ashe Devine. © 2010 by the International Reading Association.

Colonial Times Word List for a Variety of Games

1. colony
2. route
3. governor
4. slavery

5. right
6. tax
7. assembly

8. apprentice
9. diversity
10. tolerance

Directions: Select *one* of the word games below:

1. *Picture This!:* Make an illustrated picture book using *seven* of the words on the vocabulary list. Be creative, have fun, and plan to share with a friend! Use two blank sheets of paper, folded into quarters. Include a cover.

2. *Poetry Vocabulary:* Make a line poem, a definition poem, or a shape poem using *one* word from the vocabulary list. Use either lined or blank paper for your masterpiece. Examples of the poems are on the reverse side (not shown here).

3. *Clap, Tap, and Snap!:* Using *all 10* words, clap, tap, or snap the syllables for each while pronouncing each sound. Or create an imaginative, zany instrument to play during your performance (using materials available in the classroom) and sing the words.

Fun-tastic Activities for Differentiating Comprehension Instruction, Grades 2–6 by Sandra K. Athans and Denise Ashe Devine. © 2010 by the International Reading Association.

Developing Background Knowledge on Immigration and Making Connections to My World

In this activity, you'll be creating an eye-catching glyph. A glyph is visual art that conveys information about yourself. Your glyph will be about your experiences with topics we'll cover in our Immigration unit. What a great way to make connections!

Directions: Use a person pattern from the Literacy Bin (see sample on next page) and follow the legend below (just like in a map) to construct your glyph. Use other art materials available in the classroom.

Eyes	Hair	Shirt
Brown: My ancestors lived in Europe.	*Brown:* We often enjoy foods from our country of origin.	*Striped:* I can easily speak and understand the language from my country of origin.
Black: My ancestors lived in Asia.	*Red:* We don't often enjoy foods from our country of origin.	*Polka-Dot:* I can speak and understand some of the language from my country of origin.
Blue: My ancestors lived in Africa.		*Checkered:* I'm unfamiliar with the language from my country of origin (but might like to learn).
Green: My ancestors lived in another country.		

Skirt or Pants	Hat	Shoes
Striped: I've visited my country two or more times.	*Top Hat:* I've seen many books or photos on my country.	*Buckled:* I'm named after one of my ancestors.
Polka-Dot: I've visited my country one time.	*Baseball Cap:* I've seen some books or photos on my country.	*Laced:* I'm not named after an ancestor, but my name is well known in my country.
Checkered: I haven't visited my country (yet).	*Fancy Hat:* I haven't seen books or photos on my country (yet).	*Heeled:* I'm not named after an ancestor, and my name doesn't come from my country (but I really love it!).

Holding in Hand	Electronic Device	Accessories
Suitcase: We have artifacts in my home from my country.	*MP3 Player:* I know some music or can sing a song from my country.	*Earrings:* I have traditional clothing from my country of origin.
Umbrella: We do not have artifacts in my home from my country.	*PS-2 Game:* I do not know any music or songs from my country (yet).	*Necklace or Neckerchief:* I do not have traditional clothing from my country of origin.
Extra Credit: Include a flag from your country of origin in the other hand.		

Fun-tastic Activities for Differentiating Comprehension Instruction, Grades 2–6 by Sandra K. Athans and Denise Ashe Devine. © 2010 by the International Reading Association.

This sample person pattern is to be used with the glyph activity on the preceding page.

On Your Mark, Get Set Writing a RAFT, and Go!

Directions: You will be writing a RAFT using the following prompts: R represents the role you will assume as you write or read and perform your RAFT, the intended audience is A, the format you'll use is F, and the topic is T.

First Grade
Bin Theme: People in Our Community

R = village or town librarian

A = students in your class

F = an invitation

T = Invite your audience to the library. Tell two interesting things the library does for first-grade students. Also, tell one way the library helps others in the community.

Third Grade
Bin Theme: The Water Cycle

R = Mommy Rain

A = Baby Rain

F = mother's advice (can be a speech, journal entry, letter, or lullaby)

T = Inform Baby Rain what to expect as it travels through the water cycle.

Fourth Grade
Bin Theme: Tall Tales

R = tall tale character (existing or newly created)

A = other tall tale characters and the world

F = poem, speech, song, or rap

T = Inform your audience of your larger-than-life traits or features and give two examples of how you used them and the outcomes.

Sixth Grade
Bin Theme: Ancient Greece

R = Persephone

A = a modern-day police detective

F = a written description of events for a formal police record

T = Describe the events that took place during ancient times, including your abduction, your captivity in the underworld, and the effects of your ordeal on popular mythology.

Fun-tastic Activities for Differentiating Comprehension Instruction, Grades 2–6 by Sandra K. Athans and Denise Ashe Devine. © 2010 by the International Reading Association.

Reproducible Planning and Assessment Charts

The following reproducible planning and assessment charts can help you monitor your instruction and student progress:

- A Quick-Check Form
- Literacy Bin Observation Form
- Literacy Bin Portfolio Checklist
- Comprehension Practice Rubric
- Vocabulary Knowledge & Word Skills Rubric
- Background Knowledge Rubric
- Fluency Rubric
- Comprehension Practice Rubric: Writing
- Vocabulary Knowledge & Word Skills Rubric: Writing
- Background Knowledge Rubric: Writing
- Fluency Rubric: Writing
- "A Penny for Your Thoughts" Survey

A Quick-Check Form

Literacy Bin Activities

a = ***a***ccurate _____

quick = ***q***uality work _____

check = ***c***omplete _____

A Quick-Check Form

Literacy Bin Activities

a = ***a***ccurate _____

quick = ***q***uality work _____

check = ***c***omplete _____

Literacy Bin Observation of: _____ Date: _____

(Review tic-tac-toe game board and completed projects.)

- Demonstrates appropriate behavior: Yes ☐ No ☐
- Selects activities appropriately: Yes ☐ No ☐
- Uses appropriate pacing: Yes ☐ No ☐
- Works well in teams and independently: Yes ☐ No ☐
- Is self-sufficient: Yes ☐ No ☐

Comments: _____

_____

_____

Fun-tastic Activities for Differentiating Comprehension Instruction, Grades 2–6 by Sandra K. Athans and Denise Ashe Devine. © 2010 by the International Reading Association.

- -

Literacy Bin Observation of: _____ Date: _____

(Review tic-tac-toe game board and completed projects.)

- Demonstrates appropriate behavior: Yes ☐ No ☐
- Selects activities appropriately: Yes ☐ No ☐
- Uses appropriate pacing: Yes ☐ No ☐
- Works well in teams and independently: Yes ☐ No ☐
- Is self-sufficient: Yes ☐ No ☐

Comments: _____

_____

_____

Fun-tastic Activities for Differentiating Comprehension Instruction, Grades 2–6 by Sandra K. Athans and Denise Ashe Devine. © 2010 by the International Reading Association.

Literacy Bin Portfolio Checklist for: _____

Bin: _____ **Date:** _____

The work I've selected for my portfolio is:

☐ Accurate, quality work, complete!

☐ Representative of my best efforts!

☐ Unique: there's no activity like it in my portfolio!

☐ Work that makes me proud!

I wanted to share this work because: _____

_____

_____

- -

Literacy Bin Portfolio Checklist for: _____

Bin: _____ **Date:** _____

The work I've selected for my portfolio is:

☐ Accurate, quality work, complete!

☐ Representative of my best efforts!

☐ Unique: there's no activity like it in my portfolio!

☐ Work that makes me proud!

I wanted to share this work because: _____

_____

_____

Comprehension Practice Rubric

Name: _____ Date:_____

Literacy Bin Theme: _____

Activity #: _____

Demonstration of key elements of task:

_____ 4 3 2 1

_____ 4 3 2 1

_____ 4 3 2 1

_____ 4 3 2 1

Participation: _____

_____

_____

Effort: _____

_____

_____

4 = accomplished; 3 = proficient; 2 = progressing with difficulty;
1 = not progressing

Fun-tastic Activities for Differentiating Comprehension Instruction, Grades 2–6 by Sandra K. Athans
and Denise Ashe Devine. © 2010 by the International Reading Association.

Vocabulary Knowledge & Word Skills Rubric

Name: _____ Date: _____

Literacy Bin Theme: _____

Activity #: _____

Demonstration of key elements of task:

_____ 4 3 2 1

_____ 4 3 2 1

_____ 4 3 2 1

_____ 4 3 2 1

Participation: _____

_____

_____

Effort: _____

_____

_____

_____

4 = accomplished; 3 = proficient; 2 = progressing with difficulty;
1 = not progressing

Fun-tastic Activities for Differentiating Comprehension Instruction, Grades 2–6 by Sandra K. Athans and Denise Ashe Devine. © 2010 by the International Reading Association.

Background Knowledge Rubric

Name: _____ Date: _____

Literacy Bin Theme: _____

Activity #: _____

Demonstration of key elements of task:

_____ 4 3 2 1

_____ 4 3 2 1

_____ 4 3 2 1

_____ 4 3 2 1

Participation: _____

_____

_____

Effort: _____

_____

_____

_____

4 = accomplished; 3 = proficient; 2 = progressing with difficulty;
1 = not progressing

Fun-tastic Activities for Differentiating Comprehension Instruction, Grades 2–6 by Sandra K. Athans
and Denise Ashe Devine. © 2010 by the International Reading Association.

Fluency Rubric

Name: _____ Date: _____

Literacy Bin Theme: _____

Activity #: _____

Demonstration of key elements of task:

_____ 4 3 2 1

_____ 4 3 2 1

_____ 4 3 2 1

_____ 4 3 2 1

Participation: _____

_____

_____

Effort: _____

_____

_____

_____

4 = accomplished; 3 = proficient; 2 = progressing with difficulty;
1 = not progressing

Fun-tastic Activities for Differentiating Comprehension Instruction, Grades 2–6 by Sandra K. Athans
and Denise Ashe Devine. © 2010 by the International Reading Association.

Comprehension Practice
Rubric: Writing

Name: _____ Date: _____

Literacy Bin Theme: _____

Activity #: _____

Addresses the topic: Main idea is present,

task answered, understands topic, and

provides relevant written response.   4 3 2 1

Details: Develops ideas with support using

examples, connections, further description, etc.   4 3 2 1

Organization: Has a logical and orderly plan,

strong transitions, and correct paragraphing.   4 3 2 1

Mechanics: Uses correct capitalization, punctuation,

spelling, and grammar, and handwriting is legible

with letters and words formed and spaced correctly. 4 3 2 1

Effort: _____

_____

_____

4 = accomplished; 3 = proficient; 2 = progressing with difficulty;
1 = not progressing

Fun-tastic Activities for Differentiating Comprehension Instruction, Grades 2–6 by Sandra K. Athans and Denise Ashe Devine. © 2010 by the International Reading Association.

Vocabulary Knowledge & Word Skills Rubric: Writing

Name: _____ Date: _____

Literacy Bin Theme: _____

Activity #: _____

Addresses the topic: Main idea is present,

task answered, understands topic, and

provides relevant written response.   4 3 2 1

Details: Develops ideas with support using

examples, connections, further description, etc.   4 3 2 1

Organization: Has a logical and orderly plan,

strong transitions, and correct paragraphing.   4 3 2 1

Mechanics: Uses correct capitalization, punctuation,

spelling, and grammar, and handwriting is legible

with letters and words formed and spaced correctly.   4 3 2 1

Effort: _____

_____

_____

4 = accomplished; 3 = proficient; 2 = progressing with difficulty;
1 = not progressing

Fun-tastic Activities for Differentiating Comprehension Instruction, Grades 2–6 by Sandra K. Athans
and Denise Ashe Devine. © 2010 by the International Reading Association.

Background Knowledge
Rubric: Writing

Name: _____ Date: _____

Literacy Bin Theme: _____

Activity #: _____

Addresses the topic: Main idea is present,

task answered, understands topic, and

provides relevant written response.   4 3 2 1

Details: Develops ideas with support using

examples, connections, further description, etc.   4 3 2 1

Organization: Has a logical and orderly plan,

strong transitions, and correct paragraphing.   4 3 2 1

Mechanics: Uses correct capitalization, punctuation,

spelling, and grammar, and handwriting is legible

with letters and words formed and spaced correctly.   4 3 2 1

Effort: _____

_____

_____

4 = accomplished; 3 = proficient; 2 = progressing with difficulty;
1 = not progressing

Fun-tastic Activities for Differentiating Comprehension Instruction, Grades 2–6 by Sandra K. Athans
and Denise Ashe Devine. © 2010 by the International Reading Association.

Fluency Rubric: Writing

Name: _____ Date: _____

Literacy Bin Theme: _____

Activity #: _____

Addresses the topic: Main idea is present,
task answered, understands topic, and
provides relevant written response.   4 3 2 1

Details: Develops ideas with support using
examples, connections, further description, etc.   4 3 2 1

Organization: Has a logical and orderly plan,
strong transitions, and correct paragraphing.   4 3 2 1

Mechanics: Uses correct capitalization, punctuation,
spelling, and grammar, and handwriting is legible
with letters and words formed and spaced correctly.   4 3 2 1

Effort: _____

_____

_____

4 = accomplished; 3 = proficient; 2 = progressing with difficulty;
1 = not progressing

Fun-tastic Activities for Differentiating Comprehension Instruction, Grades 2–6 by Sandra K. Athans
and Denise Ashe Devine. © 2010 by the International Reading Association.

Name: _____ Date:_____

"A Penny for Your Thoughts" on the
_____ Literacy Bin!

- How many activities were you able to complete?

_____

_____

_____

- How would you rate the quality of your work? Place an X on the scale.

4	3	2	1

- Did you understand the directions for all of the activities? Were any tricky?

_____

_____

_____

- Were you able to complete the activities on your own or with a little help from classmates? Please explain.

_____

_____

_____

- Do you feel the activities in this Literacy Bin helped you? If so, how?

_____

_____

_____

- What kinds of activities would you like us to include in the next Literacy Bin?

_____

_____

_____

Fun-tastic Activities for Differentiating Comprehension Instruction, Grades 2–6 by Sandra K. Athans and Denise Ashe Devine. © 2010 by the International Reading Association.

REFERENCES

Alexander, P.A. (2006). The path to competence: A lifespan developmental perspective on reading. *Journal of Literacy Research, 37*(4), 413–436.

Allington, R.L. (1983). Fluency: The neglected reading goal. *The Reading Teacher, 36*(6), 556–561.

Applegate, M.D., Applegate, A.J., & Modla, V.B. (2009). "She's my best reader; she just can't comprehend": Studying the relationship between fluency and comprehension. *The Reading Teacher, 62*(6), 512–521. doi:10.1598/RT.62.6.5

Applegate, M.D., Quinn, K.B., & Applegate, A.J. (2008). *The critical reading inventory: Assessing students' reading and thinking* (2nd ed.). Upper Saddle River, NJ: Pearson Education.

Athans, S.K., & Devine, D.A. (2005). *Guided reading assessment strategies: Classroom research.* Unpublished report, East Syracuse: Central New York Teaching Center.

Athans, S.K., & Devine, D.A. (2008). *Quality comprehension: A strategic model of reading instruction using read-along guides, grades 3–6.* Newark, DE: International Reading Association.

Athans, S.K., & Devine, D.A. (2009). *Motivating every student in literacy (including the highly unmotivated!), grades 3–6.* Larchmont, NY: Eye on Education.

Athans, S.K., Devine, D.A., Henry, D., & Sammon, K. (2007). *Literacy bins: Best practices and strategic support classroom research.* East Syracuse: Central New York Teaching Center.

Beck, I.L., McKeown, M.G., & Kucan, L. (2002). *Bringing words to life: Robust vocabulary instruction.* New York: Guilford.

Beck, I.L., McKeown, M.G., & Kucan, L. (2008). *Creating robust vocabulary: Frequently asked questions and extended examples.* New York: Guilford.

Blachowicz, C.L.Z., & Fisher, P.J. (2004). Keep the "fun" in fundamental: Encouraging word awareness and incidental word learning in the classroom through word play. In J.F. Baumann & E.J. Kame'enui (Eds.), *Vocabulary instruction: Research to practice* (pp. 218–237). New York: Guilford.

Brozo, W.G., & Flynt, E.S. (2008). Motivating students to read in the content classroom: Six evidence-based principles. *The Reading Teacher, 62*(2), 172–174. doi:10.1598/RT.62.2.9

Brozo, W.G., & Simpson, M.L. (2007). *Content literacy for today's adolescents: Honoring diversity and building competence* (5th ed.). Upper Saddle River, NJ: Merrill/Prentice Hall.

Chall, J.S., & Jacobs, V.A. (2003). Poor children's fourth-grade slump. *American Educator, 27*(1), 14–15, 44.

Cunningham, A.E., & Stanovich, K.E. (1997). Early reading acquisition and its relation to reading experience and ability 10 years later. *Developmental Psychology, 33*(6), 934–945. doi:10.1037/0012-1649.33.6.934

Deci, E.L., & Ryan, R.M. (1985). *Intrinsic motivation and self-determination in human behavior.* New York: Plenum.

Dochy, F., Segers, M., & Buehl, M.M. (1999). The relation between assessment practices and outcomes of studies: The case of research on prior knowledge. *Review of Educational Research, 69*(2), 145–186.

Dochy, F.J.R.C., & Alexander, P.A. (1995). Mapping prior knowledge: A framework for discussion among researchers. *European Journal of Psychology of Education, 10*(3), 225–242.

Flynt, E.S., & Brozo, W.G. (2008). Developing academic language: Got words? *The Reading Teacher, 61*(6), 500–502. doi:10.1598/RT.61.6.9

Ford, M.E. (1992). *Motivating humans: Goals, emotions, and personal agency beliefs.* Newbury Park, CA: Sage.

Fountas, I.C., & Pinnell, G.S. (1996). *Guided reading: Good first teaching for all children.* Portsmouth, NH: Heinemann.

Fountas, I.C., & Pinnell, G.S. (2001). *Guiding readers and writers, grades 3–6: Teaching comprehension, genre, and content literacy.* Portsmouth, NH: Heinemann.

Fountas, I.C., & Pinnell, G.S. (2006). *Teaching for comprehending and fluency: Thinking, talking, and writing about reading, K–8.* Portsmouth, NH: Heinemann.

Fountas, I.C., & Pinnell, G.S. (2008). *Fountas & Pinnell benchmark assessment system 2: Assessment guide.* Portsmouth, NH: Heinemann.

Gambrell, L.B., Morrow, L.M., & Pressley, M. (2007). *Best practices in literacy instruction* (3rd ed.). New York: Guilford.

Gambrell, L.B., Palmer, B.M., Codling, R.M., & Mazzoni, S.A. (1996). Assessing motivation to read. *The Reading Teacher, 49*(7), 518–533. doi:10.1598/RT.49.7.2

Gardner, H. (1983). *Frames of mind: The theory of multiple intelligences.* New York: Basic.

Gardner, H. (1999). *Intelligence reframed: Multiple intelligences for the 21st century.* New York: Basic.

Gardner, H., & Moran, S. (2006). The science of multiple intelligences theory: A response to Lynn Waterhouse. *Educational Psychologist, 41*(4), 227–232. doi:10.1207/s15326985ep4104_2

Graves, M.F. (2006). *The vocabulary book: Learning and instruction.* New York: Teachers College Press; Newark, DE: International Reading Association.

Guastello, E.F., & Lenz, C.R. (2007). *The guided reading kidstation model: Making instruction meaningful for the whole class.* Newark, DE: International Reading Association.

Guthrie, J.T., & Wigfield, A. (1997). Reading engagement: A rationale for theory and teaching. In J.T. Guthrie & A. Wigfield (Eds.), *Reading engagement: Motivating readers through integrated instruction* (pp. 1–12). Newark, DE: International Reading Association.

Harmon, J.M., Hedrick, W.B., & Wood, K.D. (2005). Research on vocabulary instruction in the content areas: Implications for struggling readers. *Reading & Writing Quarterly, 21*(3), 261–280. doi:10.1080/10573560590949377

Harris, T.L., & Hodges, R.E. (Eds.). (1995). *The literacy dictionary: The vocabulary of reading and writing.* Newark, DE: International Reading Association.

Harvey, S., & Goudvis, A. (2000). *Strategies that work: Teaching comprehension to enhance understanding.* Portland, ME: Stenhouse.

Hasbrouck, J.E., & Tindal, G. (1992). Curriculum-based oral reading fluency norms for students in grades 2 through 5. *Teaching Exceptional Children, 24*(3), 41–44.

Hasbrouck, J.E., & Tindal, G. (2006). 2006 Hasbrouck & Tindal oral reading fluency data. St. Paul, MN: Read Naturally. Retrieved October 15, 2009, from www.readnaturally .com/pdf/oralreadingfluency.pdf

Hirsch, E.D., Jr. (2006). The case for bringing content into the language arts block and for a knowledge-rich curriculum core for all children. *American Educator, 30*(1). Retrieved November 10, 2009, from www.aft.org/pubs-reports/american_educator/issues/ spring06/hirsch.htm

Jung, C. (1927). *The theory of psychological type.* Princeton, NJ: Princeton University Press.

Kajder, S.B. (2006). *Bringing the outside in: Visual ways to engage reluctant readers.* Portland, ME: Stenhouse.

Kamil, M.L., & Hiebert, E.H. (2005). Teaching and learning vocabulary: Perspectives and persistent issues. In E.H. Hiebert & M.L. Kamil (Eds.), *Teaching and learning vocabulary: Bringing research to practice* (pp. 1–23). Mahwah, NJ: Erlbaum.

Keene, E.O., & Zimmermann, S. (2007). *Mosaic of thought: The power of comprehension strategy instruction* (2nd ed.). Portsmouth, NH: Heinemann.

Kieffer, M.J., & Lesaux, N.K. (2007). Breaking down words to build meaning: Morphology, vocabulary, and reading comprehension in the urban classroom. *The Reading Teacher, 61*(2), 134–144. doi:10.1598/RT.61.2.3

LaBerge, D., & Samuels, S.J. (1974). Toward a theory of automatic information processing in reading. *Cognitive Psychology, 6,* 293–323.

Langer, J.A. (1984). Examining background knowledge and text comprehension. *Reading Research Quarterly, 19*(4), 468–481.

Lavoie, R.D. (2007). *The motivation breakthrough: 6 secrets to turning on the tuned-out child.* New York: Touchstone.

Lenz, B.K. (2005, October). *Building background knowledge for literacy: Tying standards-based planning to inclusive teaching.* Keynote address for the International Council for Learning Disabilities, Ft. Lauderdale, FL. Retrieved November 10, 2009, from www.kucrl.org/library/presentations/icld2005.pdf

Lepper, M.R. (1988). Motivational considerations in the study of instruction. *Cognition and Instruction, 5*(4), 289–309. doi:10.1207/s1532690xci0504_3

Leu, D.J. (2006). New literacies, reading research, and the challenges of change: A deictic perspective. In J.V. Hoffman, D.L. Schallert, C.M. Fairbanks, J. Worthy, & B. Maloch (Eds.), *55th yearbook of the National Reading Conference* (pp. 1–20). Oak Creek, WI: National Reading Conference.

Long, S.A., Winograd, P.N., & Bridge, C.A. (1989). The effects of reader and text characteristics on imagery reported during and after reading. *Reading Research Quarterly, 24*(3), 353–372.

Maehr, M.L. (1976). Continuing motivation: An analysis of a seldom considered educational outcome. *Review of Educational Research, 46*(3), 443–462.

Mendler, A.N. (2000). *Motivating students who don't care: Successful techniques for educators.* Bloomington, IN: Solution Tree.

Monroe, J. (2002, April). *Guided reading: Teaching strategies for grades 3–8.* Paper presented at a seminar sponsored by Staff Development Resources, Syracuse, NY.

Nagy, W.E., & Anderson, R.C. (1984). How many words are there in printed school English? *Reading Research Quarterly, 19*(3), 304–330. doi:10.2307/747823

National Institute of Child Health and Human Development. (2000). *Report of the National Reading Panel. Teaching children to read: An evidence-based assessment of the scientific research literature on reading and its implications for reading instruction* (NIH Publication No. 00–4769). Washington, DC: U.S. Government Printing Office.

Ness, M. (2009). Laughing through rereadings: Using joke books to build fluency. *The Reading Teacher, 62*(8), 691–694. doi:10.1598/RT.62.8.7

Padak, N., & Rasinski, T. (2005). *Fast start for early readers.* New York: Scholastic.

Palincsar, A.S., & Brown, A.L. (1984). Reciprocal teaching of comprehension-fostering and comprehension-monitoring activities. *Cognition and Instruction, 1*(2), 117–175.

Paris, S.G., & Oka, E.R. (1986). Self-regulated learning among exceptional children. *Exceptional Children, 53*(2), 103–108.

Pearson, P.D., & Fielding, L. (1996). Comprehension instruction. In R. Barr, M.L. Kamil, P. Mosenthal, & P.D. Pearson (Eds.), *Handbook of reading research* (Vol. 2, pp. 815–860). Mahwah, NJ: Erlbaum.

Pearson, P.D., & Gallagher, M.C. (1983). The instruction of reading comprehension. *Contemporary Educational Psychology, 8*(3), 317–344.

Peebles, J.L. (2007). Incorporating movement with fluency instruction: A motivation for struggling readers. *The Reading Teacher, 60*(6), 578–581. doi:10.1598/RT.60.6.9

Pinnell, G.S., & Fountas, I.C. (2002). *Leveled books for readers, grades 3–6: A companion volume to* Guiding Readers and Writers. Portsmouth, NH: Heinemann.

RAND Reading Study Group. (2002). *Reading for understanding: Toward an R&D program in reading comprehension.* Santa Monica, CA: RAND.

Rasinski, T.V. (2003). *The fluent reader: Oral reading strategies for building word recognition, fluency, and comprehension.* New York: Scholastic.

Rasinski, T.V. (2006). Reading fluency instruction: Moving beyond accuracy, automaticity, and prosody. *The Reading Teacher, 59*(7), 704–706. doi:10.1598/RT.59.7.10

Reading A–Z. (n.d.). Fluency standards table: Recommendations. Retrieved October 15, 2009, from www.readinga-z.com/fluency/index.html

Sagor, R. (2003). *Motivating students and teachers in an era of standards.* Alexandria, VA: Association for Supervision and Curriculum Development.

Samblis, K. (2006). Think-tac-toe, a motivating method of increasing comprehension. *The Reading Teacher, 59*(7), 691–694. doi:10.1598/RT.59.7.8

Santa, C.M. (with Havens, L., Nelson, M., Danner, M., Scalf, L., & Scalf, J.). (1988). *Content reading including study systems: Reading, writing and studying across the curriculum.* Dubuque, IA: Kendall/Hunt.

Schunk, D.H. (1985). Self-efficacy and classroom learning. *Psychology in the Schools, 22*(2), 208–223.

Snow, C.E., Tabors, P.O., Nicholson, P.A., & Kurland, B.F. (1995). SHELL: Oral language and early literacy skills in kindergarten and first-grade children. *Journal of Research in Childhood Education, 10*(1), 37–47.

Stahl, S.A., & Nagy, W.E. (2006). *Teaching word meanings.* Mahwah, NJ: Erlbaum.

Stanley, N. (2004). A celebration of words. *Teaching Pre K–8, 34*(7), 56–57.

Sternberg, R.J. (2000). Patterns of giftedness: A triarchic analysis. *Roeper Review, 22*(4), 231–235.

Stevens, K.C. (1980). The effect of background knowledge on the reading comprehension of ninth graders. *Journal of Reading Behavior, 12*(2), 151–154.

Stix, A., & Hrbek, F. (2006). *Teachers as classroom coaches: How to motivate students across the content areas.* Alexandria, VA: Association for Supervision and Curriculum Development.

Strickland, D.S., Ganske, K., & Monroe, J.K. (2002). *Supporting struggling readers and writers: Strategies for classroom intervention, 3–6.* Portland, ME: Stenhouse; Newark, DE: International Reading Association.

Tobias, S. (1994). Interest, prior knowledge, and learning. *Review of Educational Research, 64*(1), 37–54.

Tomlinson, C.A. (2004). *How to differentiate instruction in mixed-ability classrooms* (2nd ed.). Alexandria, VA: Association for Supervision and Curriculum Development.

Tomlinson, C.A. (Speaker). (2009, May 15). *Exploring differentiated instruction* [Online chat]. Bethesda, MD: Education Week. Retrieved May 15, 2009, from www.edweek.org/ew/events/chats/2009/05/15/index.html

van Klaveren, K., Buckland, T., Williamson, J.L., Kunselman, M.M., Wilkinson, J., & Cunningham, S. (2002). How do your students learn? *Science Scope, 25*(7), 24–29.

Wagner, R.K., Torgesen, J.K., Rashotte, C.A., Hecht, S.A., Barker, T.A., Burgess, S.R., et al. (1997). Changing relations between phonological processing abilities and word-level reading as children develop from beginning to skilled readers: A 5-year longitudinal study. *Developmental Psychology, 33*(3), 468–479. doi:10.1037/0012-1649.33.3.468

Willingham, D.T. (2007). Should learning be its own reward? *American Educator, 31*(4), 29–35, 47.

Yopp, R.H., & Yopp, H.K. (2007). Ten important words plus: A strategy for building word knowledge. *The Reading Teacher, 61*(2), 157–160. doi:10.1598/RT.61.2.5

Zimmermann, S., & Hutchins, C. (2003). *7 keys to comprehension: How to help your kids read it and get it!* New York: Three Rivers Press.

Zutell, J., & Rasinski, T.V. (1991). Training teachers to attend to their students' oral reading fluency. *Theory Into Practice, 30*(3), 211–217.

LITERATURE CITED

Dalgliesh, A. (1954). *The courage of Sarah Noble.* New York: Scribner.

INDEX

Note. The designations *f* and *t* refer to page numbers of figures and tables, respectively.

A

ABC bookmark activity, 86, 86*f*
advice activities: fluency-related, 102, 102*f*; for vocabulary and word skills, 69–70, 70*f*
Alexander, P.A., xiv, 77, 78
Allen, J., 72
Allen, M.B., 56
Allington, R.L., 89, 102
ancient Greece theme, 141
Anderson, R.C., 59
Applegate, A.J., 90, 92
Applegate, M.D., 90, 92
articles: for comprehension practice, 56; fluency-related, 87, 103; vocabulary and word-building resource materials, 73
assessing student activities: about, 112; Background Knowledge Rubric, 116*f*, 149; Background Knowledge Rubric: Writing, 117*f*, 153; Comprehension Practice Rubric, 116*f*, 147; Comprehension Practice Rubric: Writing, 117*f*, 151; Fluency Rubric, 116*f*, 150; Fluency Rubric: Writing, 117*f*, 154; oral presentation and listening skills, 114*t*; "A Penny for Your Thoughts" Survey, 119*f*, 155; Portfolio Checklist, 112–114, 113*f*, 146; targeted rubrics, 115–118, 116*f*–117*f*; using students' views for, 118–120, 119*f*; Vocabulary Knowledge & Word Skills Rubric, 116*f*, 148; Vocabulary Knowledge & Word Skills Rubric: Writing, 117*f*, 152
Athans, S.K., vii–viii, xii, xiii, xvi, 32, 41, 42, 55, 77, 90, 111, 126–141, 144–155
atozteacherstuff.com, 73
auditory learners: defined, 7; mixing activity types, 20*f*
autonomy: selecting Literacy Bin Activities, 27–31, 29*f*; student motivation and, 4–5

B

background knowledge: ABC bookmark activity, 86, 86*f*; Background Knowledge Rubric, 116*f*, 149; Background Knowledge Rubric: Writing, 117*f*, 153; building, 13; comic book writer activity, 84–85, 84*f*; crafting RAFTs, 85–86, 85*f*; create a museum activity, 81, 81*f*; create a rap activity, 84, 84*f*; create a slideshow activity, 83, 83*f*; defined, 78; fact or fiction card game, 82–83, 83*f*; Genius TV Talk Show script, 23*f*; glyphs activity, 81–82, 82*f*; Immigration Background Knowledge Glyph (Directions), 139–140; importance of, 78–80; Literacy Bin Activities to enhance, 80–86; mixing activity types, 20*f*; mock trial activity, 85, 85*f*; perform a Readers Theatre script, 83, 83*f*; postcard from... activity, 84, 84*f*; read at home activity, 81, 81*f*; resource materials for, 86–87; teachers suggesting activities, 29–30; web work activity, 82, 82*f*
Baumann, J.F., 72
Beck, I.L., 59, 60, 62, 72
blab sheets, 96, 96*f*
Blachowicz, C.L.Z., 62, 72
blank tic-tac-toe game board, 126
Block, C.C., 72
bodily/kinesthetic intelligence: activities targeting, 8*t*; mixing activity types, 20*f*; in multiple intelligence model, 5, 6
book-format and graphic organizers for vocabulary and word skills, 70, 70*f*
bookmark activity, 86, 86*f*
books as resource materials: background knowledge-related, 87; for comprehension practice, 55–56; fluency-related, 102–103; vocabulary and word-building resource materials, 72
Bosco, D., 135

Bridge, C.A., 79
Bringing Words to Life (Beck, McKeown, and Kucan), 72
Brooks, C., 136
Brown, A.L., 42
Brozo, W.G., 59, 60, 90–92
Buehl, M.M., 79
Building Background Knowledge for Academic Achievement (Marzano), 87

C

canon sing-along activity, 98, 98*f*
cause-and-effect relationships, 53, 53*f*
Chall, J.S., 59
cheer activity, 99–100, 100*f*
choice: selecting Literacy Bin Activities, 27–31, 29*f*; student motivation and, 4–5
Codling, R.M., xv
collaboration in choosing student peers, 31
Colonial times unit: sample directions for word activities, 138; tic-tac-toe board game, 3*f*, 129
comic book writer activity: for background knowledge, 84–85, 84*f*; sample directions for, 25*f*; in tic-tac-toe game board example, 18, 18*f*
comical characters for word-attack skills, 69, 69*f*
community unit: directions for writing RAFTs, 141; tic-tac-toe board game for, 133
compare and contrast ideas in strategy-based instruction, 52, 52*f*
comprehension skills: building strategy-based instruction, 45–54; comprehension practice resource materials, 54–57; Comprehension Practice Rubric, 116*f*, 147; Comprehension Practice Rubric: Writing, 117*f*, 151; foundational eight strategies, 46–50, 46*f*–50*f*; mixing activity types, 20*f*; quality comprehension model, 42–45; relationship between fluency and, 92; relationship between vocabulary and, 60–61; resource materials for, 54–56; skill-building nine strategies for, 50–54, 50*f*–54*f*; strategy-

based comprehension, 41–42, 45; supplementing instruction, 13
conclusions, drawing, 53–54, 54*f*
Connection Caboodle card game, 48, 48*f*
The Courage of Sarah Noble (Dalgliesh), xii–xiii
courtesy tips, creating, 25–26
Creating Robust Vocabulary (Beck, McKeown, and Kucan), 72
creative competitions activity, 67, 67*f*
creative connections activity, 69, 69*f*
Cunningham, A.E., 60
Curriculum Associates, 55

D

Dalgliesh, Alice, xii–xiii
Deci, E.L., xv
Devine, D.A., viii, xii, xiii, xvi, 32, 41, 42, 55, 77, 90, 111, 126–141, 144–155
dictionary and glossary skills, 61
differentiated instruction, 10–11
Dochy, F.J.R.C., 78, 79
drama activities: for fluency development, 100–101, 100*f*; Genius TV Talk Show, 39; vocabulary and word skills in, 65–66, 66*f*
drawing activities, 65, 65*f*
Dunn and Dunn learning styles model, 7

E

edhelper.com, 73
existentialism, 5
extension activities, xvi

F

facts: distinguishing from opinions, 51, 51*f*; fact or fiction? card game activity, 82–83, 83*f*; identifying, 50–51, 51*f*
fantasy activities, 98–99, 99*f*
Farstrup, A.E., 103
Fielding, L., 79
figurative language, interpreting, 52–53, 53*f*
finger and movement rhyme activities, 97, 97*f*
Fingeret, L., 103
Fisher, P.J., 62, 72
FitzGibbons, D., 137
fix-up methods in strategy-based instruction, 46, 46*f*

fluency: advice activities, 102, 102*f*; canon sing-along activity, 98, 98*f*; create a cheer activity, 99–100, 100*f*; defining, 89–90; developing, 14; developing with Readers Theatre script, 93, 93*f*; fantasy activities, 98–99, 99*f*; finger and movement rhyme activities, 97, 97*f*; Fluency Rubric, 116*f*, 150; Fluency Rubric: Writing, 117*f*, 154; Genius TV Talk Show script, 23, 23*f*; grade level recommendations, 91*t*; how-to demonstrations, 101, 101*f*; imaginative challenges activity, 97, 97*f*; imaginative characters activity, 98, 98*f*; imaginative games activity, 99, 99*f*; importance of, 90–93; jump rope jingles and routines activity, 100, 100*f*; Literacy Bin Activities to develop, 93–102; mixing activity types, 20*f*; oral reading rates, 91*t*; perform a speech activity, 94–95, 94*f*; present a monologue or soliloquy activity, 95–96, 95*f*; puppet show activity, 96, 96*f*; read-aloud storytelling activity, 94, 94*f*; reciting poetry, 93–94, 94*f*; related resource materials, 102–103; relationship between comprehension and, 92; sign of the times activity, 96, 96*f*; simulations and dramatic play activity, 100–101, 100*f*; sing a song activity, 95, 95*f*; teachers suggesting activities, 29–30; timing activities, 101, 101*f*; words-per-minute guidelines, 91*t*
The Fluent Reader (Rasinski), 103
Flynt, E.S., 59, 90–92
Ford, M.E., xv
Fountas, I.C., xii, 21, 22, 41, 55, 56, 89, 90, 91, 103
Fountas & Pinnell Benchmark Assessment System 2, 103
Frames of Mind (Gardner), 5
Fry, E., 103

G
Gallagher, M.C., 42
Gambrell, L.B., xv, 4
game boards. *See also* tic-tac-toe game boards: creating, 19–22; grids illustrating different mixes of activity types, 20*f*; repurposing, 39
Ganske, K., xii, 56
Gardner, H., 5–7
Gaskins, I., 103
Genalo, D., 137
Genius TV Talk Show: as drama activity, 39; fluency activity, 23, 23*f*; writing interview questions for, 48
glyphs activity: for background knowledge, 81–82, 82*f*; Immigration Background Knowledge Glyph (Directions), 139–140
Goudvis, A., xii, xvi, 41, 56
grading Literacy Bin Activities, 123
gradual release of responsibility model, 42–44
Graves, M.F., 59, 60, 72
Greek and Latin Roots (Rasinski, Padak, Newton, and Newton), 72
Guastello, E.F., 25
Guided Comprehension (McLaughlin and Allen), 56
Guided Comprehension in Action (McLaughlin), 56
Guided Reading (Fountas and Pinnell), 55
guided reading instruction, 41–42, 44
Guiding Readers and Writers, Grades 3–6 (Fountas and Pinnell), 55
Guthrie, J.T., xv, 4

H
Hanifin, J., 135
Harmon, J.M., 61
Harris, T.L., 90
Harvey, S., xii, xvi, 41, 56
Hasbrouck, J.E., 89, 91
Hedrick, W.B., 61
Henry, D., 90
Hiebert, E.H., 59
Hirsch, E.D., Jr., 78
Hodges, R.E., 90
how-to demonstrations, 101, 101*f*
Hrbek, F., xv
Hutchins, C., 42, 87

I
ideas: comparing and contrasting activity, 52, 52*f*; identifying main, 50, 50*f*; for Literacy Bin Activities, 122

imaginative challenges activity, 97, 97*f*
imaginative characters activity, 64*f*, 98, 98*f*
imaginative games activity, 99, 99*f*
imaginative phonetics activity, 63, 63*f*
imaginative word games activity, 64–65, 64*f*
immigration and the Erie Canal unit: classroom space, location, and time considerations, 32; sample directions for, 139–140; tic-tac-toe board game for, 18*f*, 131
incidental word learning, 59
Increasing Fluency With High Frequency Word Phrases Grade 2 (Rasinski, Fry, and Knoblock), 103
independent learning: encouraging, 1–12; with Literacy Bin Activities, 121
inferences, making, 53–54, 54*f*
intelligence: defining, 5; Dunn and Dunn learning styles model, 7; Lowry true colors model, 7; multiple intelligence model, 5–7, 8*t*–9*t*; triarchic theory of human intelligence, 7; visual-auditory-kinesthetic model, 7
International Reading Association, 73
interpersonal intelligence: activities targeting, 9*t*; mixing activity types, 20*f*; in multiple intelligence model, 5, 6
interpreting figurative language, 52–53, 53*f*
intrapersonal intelligence: activities targeting, 9*t*; in multiple intelligence model, 5, 6

J
Jacobs, V.A., 59
jump rope jingles and routines activity, 100, 100*f*
Jung, C., 5

K
Kajder, S.B., 10
Kame'enui, E.J., 72
Kamil, M.L., 59
Keene, E.O., xii, 41, 56, 78, 87
Kieffer, M.J., 60
kinesthetic learners: defined, 7; mixing activity types, 20*f*

Knoblock, K., 103
Kucan, L., 59, 60, 72
Kurland, B.F., 60

L
LaBerge, D., 90
Langer, J.A., 79
language arts curriculum, 14–15
Lavoie, R.D., xv
learning styles and preferences: differentiated instruction and, 10–11; multiple intelligence model, 5–7; student motivation and, 5–9
Lenz, B.K., 77
Lenz, C.R., 25
Lepper, M.R., xv
Lesaux, N.K., 60
Leu, D.J., 15
listening skills, 114*t*
Literacy Bin Activities. *See also* specific activities: about, xviii–xix, 2–4; to build vocabulary and word skills, 63–71; for building strategy-based instruction, 45–54; classroom space, location, and time considerations, 31–33; to develop fluency, 93–102; difficulty completing, 122–123; encouraging independent learning, 1–12; to enhance background knowledge, 80–86; frequency of activities, 122; frequency of changing, 121; frequently asked questions, 121–123; getting ideas and materials for, 122; grading, 123; implementation model for, 38*t*; improving, 123; incorporating with required work, 123; incorporating with thematic units, 14–18; introducing students to, 25–27; within a larger framework of instruction, 13–14; making and locating materials, 19–22; motivating students, 1–12; resource materials, 37–40; reusing, 121; selecting activities, 27–31, 29*f*; selecting additional materials, 22–27; step-by-step guidance, 33–37; time considerations, 122; tips for creating, 122; topic considerations, 121; working independently on, 121; wow appeal, 11–12
Literacy Bin Library, 24, 24*f*–25*f*

Literacy Bin Observation Form, 109–111, 109*f*, 145
Literacy Bin Portfolio Checklist, 112–114, 113*f*, 146
logical/mathematical intelligence: activities targeting, 8*t*; mixing activity types, 20*f*; in multiple intelligence model, 5, 6
Long, S.A., 79
Lowry true colors model, 7

M
Maehr, M.L., xv
Mangieri, J.N., 72
Marzano, R.J., 87
Mazzoni, S.A., xv
McEwan, E.K., 87
McKeown, M.G., 59, 60, 72
McLaughlin, M., 56
meiosis and mitosis thematic unit, 19
Mendler, A.N., xv
mock trial activity, 85, 85*f*
Modla, V.B., 92
monitoring techniques: importance of, 105–106; Literacy Bin Observation Form, 109–111, 109*f*, 145; need for extensive, 111; "A Penny for Your Thoughts" Survey, 119*f*, 155; A Quick-Check Form, 26, 107*f*, 144; quick check system, 106–108; using students' views for, 118–120, 119*f*
monologue activity, 95–96, 95*f*
Monroe, J.K., xii, 41, 56
Moran, S., 5
Morrow, L.M., 4
Mosaic of Thought (Keene and Zimmermann), 56, 87
motivation. *See* student motivation
motivation bins, xvi
multiple intelligences model, 5–7, 8*t*–9*t*
museum activity, 81, 81*f*
musical intelligence: activities targeting, 9*t*; mixing activity types, 20*f*; in multiple intelligence model, 5, 6
My Prairie Year (Plaisted), 22*f*

N
Nagy, W.E., 59, 72
National Council of Teachers of English, 73

National Institute of Child Health and Human Development [NICHD], 59, 89
national standards: background knowledge-related resource materials, 86–87; comprehension practice resource materials, 54–55; fluency-related resource materials, 102; vocabulary and word-building resource materials, 71
Native Americans unit (tic-tac-toe board game), 128
naturalist intelligence: activities targeting, 9*t*; mixing activity types, 20*f*; in multiple intelligence model, 5, 6
Ness, M., 92
Newton, E., 72
Newton, R.M., 72
Nicholson, P.A., 60
No Child Left Behind regulations, 15

O
Oczkus, L.D., 56
Oka, E.R., 16
online resources: background knowledge-related, 88; for comprehension practice, 57; fluency-related, 103; vocabulary and word-building-related, 66, 66*f*, 73
oral presentation skills: assessing, 114*t*; monologue or soliloquy activity, 95–96, 95*f*; speech activity, 94–95, 94*f*

P
Padak, N., 62, 72
Palincsar, A.S., 42
Palmer, B.M., xv
Paris, S.G., 16
Pearson, P.D., 42, 79
Peebles, J.L., 92
peer partnerships, 21, 31
"A Penny for Your Thoughts" Survey, 119*f*, 155
people in our community theme, 141
person pattern, 140
phonetics activity, 63, 63*f*
Pinnell, G.S., xii, 21, 22, 41, 55, 56, 89, 90, 91, 103
plants unit (tic-tac-toe board game), 134

poetry: fluency activity, 93–94, 94*f*; vocabulary and word skills activity, 68, 68*f*

Portfolio Checklist, 112–114, 113*f*, 146

postcard from... activity, 84, 84*f*

predictions, making, 49, 49*f*

Pressley, M., 4, 103

prior knowledge. *See* background knowledge

puppet show activity, 96, 96*f*

Q

Quality Comprehension (Athans and Devine), 55

Quality Comprehension Model: about, xii, 42–45; comprehension strategies of, 43*t*–44*t*

question asking in strategy-based instruction, 47–48, 48*f*

quick-check system: about, 106–108; A Quick-Check Form, 26, 107*f*, 144

Quinn, K.B., 90

R

RAFTs: crafting for background knowledge, 85–86, 85*f*; directions for writing, 141; reciting poetry, 94

RAND Reading Study Group, 59, 61

rap activity, 84, 84*f*

Rasinski, T.V., 62, 72, 89, 90, 91, 92, 103

Read-Along Guide: about, xii–xiv; example, xiii; Quality Comprehension Model and, 44; vocabulary and word skills and, 61

read-aloud performance: for fluency development, 94, 94*f*; mixing activity types, 20*f*

read at home activity: for background knowledge, 81, 81*f*; mixing activity types, 20*f*; sample instructions, 22*f*

Readers Theatre: background knowledge activity, 83, 83*f*; developing fluency, 92, 93, 93*f*; mixing activity types, 20*f*; monitoring technique for, 108; performing scripts, 83; resource material availability, 39

reading fluency. *See* fluency

readinga-z.com, 91

ReadWriteThink.org, 73

Reciprocal Teaching at Work (Oczkus), 56

resource materials: for background knowledge, 86–87; for building vocabulary and word skills, 71–74; for comprehension practice, 54–57; fluency-related, 102–103; for Literacy Bin Activities, 37–40

Revolutionary period and the New Nation unit: classroom space, location, and time considerations, 32; tic-tac-toe board game for, 17*f*, 130

Ryan, R.M., xv

S

Sagor, R., xv, 4

Samblis, K., xvi

Sammon, K., 90

Samuels, S.J., 90, 103

Santa, C.M., 85

Sarah, Plain and Tall (MacLachlan), 22*f*

scaffolding. *See* background knowledge

Schunk, D.H., 16

science curriculum, 16

Segers, M., 79

self-directed study, 26, 30, 30*f*, 121

sequence, understanding, 51–52, 52*f*

7 Keys to Comprehension (Zimmermann and Hutchins), 42, 87

sign of the times activity, 96, 96*f*

Simpson, M.L., 60

simulations and dramatic play activity, 100–101, 100*f*

sing a song activity, 95, 95*f*

sing-along activity, 98, 98*f*

slideshow activity, 83, 83*f*

Snow, C.E., 60

social studies curriculum, 16

soliloquy activity, 95–96, 95*f*

sorting activity, 67, 67*f*

speech activity, 94–95, 94*f*

spelling: spelling and word close-ups activity, 65, 65*f*; tic-tac-toe board game for, 137

Stahl, S.A., 59, 72

Stanley, N., 92

Stanovich, K.E., 60

state assessments: comprehension practice resource materials, 55; vocabulary and word-building resource materials, 71–72 state standards: background knowledge-related resource materials, 86–87; comprehension practice resource materials, 54–55; fluency-related resource materials, 102; vocabulary and word-building resource materials, 71

Sternberg, R.J., 7

Stevens, K.C., 79

Stix, A., xv

Strategies That Work (Harvey and Goudvis), 56

Strategies to Achieve Reading Success (Curriculum Associates), 55

strategy-based instruction: for cause-and-effect relationships, 53, 53*f*; for compare and contrast ideas, 52, 52*f*; on distinguishing fact from opinion, 51, 51*f*; on drawing conclusions, 53–54, 54*f*; fix-up methods in, 46, 46*f*; guided reading and, 41–42, 44–45; on identifying facts and details, 50–51, 51*f*; on identifying main ideas, 50, 50*f*; importance of, 45; on interpreting figurative language, 52–53, 53*f*; Literacy Bin Activities for building, 45–54; on making inferences, 53–54, 54*f*; on making predictions, 49, 49*f*; Quality Comprehension Model and, 43*t*–44*t*; question asking in, 47–48, 48*f*; on summarizing, 54, 54*f*; on synthesizing knowledge, 49–50, 50*f*; on understanding sequence, 51–52, 52*f*; on visualization, 48–49, 49*f*; for vocabulary and word skills, 46–47, 47*f*

Strickland, D.S., xii, 56

student motivation: choice and autonomy in, 4–5, 27–31; differentiated instruction and, 10–11; encouraging independent learning, 1–12; importance of, xiv–xvii; learning styles and preferences, 5–9; power of, 4–11

summarizing in strategy-based instruction, 54, 54*f*

Supporting Struggling Readers and Writers (Strickland, Ganske, and Monroe), 56

surveys, 119*f*, 155

swap-out cards, 30, 30*f*

syllabification snap-alongs and, 64, 64*f*

synthesizing knowledge, 49–50, 50*f*

T

Tabors, P.O., 60

tall tales unit: directions for writing RAFTs, 141; tic-tac-toe board game for, 127

Teaching for Comprehending and Fluency (Fountas and Pinnell), 103

Teaching for Comprehension (Fountas and Pinnell), 56

Teaching Vocabulary in All Classrooms (Blachowitz and Fisher), 72

Teaching Word Meanings (Stahl and Nagy), 72

technology: integrating into classrooms, 12; mixing activity types, 20*f*; recording student activities, 113–114

textbook selections, 72

thematic units. *See also* specific units: incorporating activities with, 14–19; suggested topics, 16*t*

tic-tac-toe game boards: blank form, 126; choosing order of completing activities, 31; for literacy, 136; for spelling, 137; students choosing activities and, 27–28; for unit on Colonial times, 3*f*, 129; for unit on community, 133; for unit on Earth's surface, 135; for unit on immigration and the Erie Canal, 18*f*, 32, 131; for unit on Native Americans, 128; for unit on plants, 134; for unit on tall tales, 127; for unit on the Revolutionary period and the New Nation, 17*f*, 32, 130; for unit on the U.S. presidents, 132

timing word count activities, 101, 101*f*

Tindal, G., 89, 91

Tobias, S., 79

Tomlinson, C.A., 4, 10, 11

trading cards activity, 66, 66*f*

triarchic theory of human intelligence, 7

U

unique sorting activity, 67, 67*f*

unique word jumbles activity, 67–68, 67*f*

U.S. presidents unit (tic-tac-toe board game), 132

Use Easy Nonfiction to Build Background Knowledge (McEwan), 87

V

van Klaveren, K., 5, 7

Venn diagrams, 52

verbal/linguistic intelligence: activities targeting, 8*t*; mixing activity types, 20*f*; in multiple intelligence model, 5, 6

visual-auditory-kinesthetic model, 7

visual learners: defined, 7; strategy-based instruction for, 47, 47*f*

visual/spatial intelligence: activities targeting, 8*t*; mixing activity types, 20*f*; in multiple intelligence model, 5, 6

visualization in strategy-based instruction, 48–49, 49*f*

vocabulary and word skills: activities with word manipulatives, 70–71, 70*f*; advice activities, 69–70, 70*f*; comical characters for word-attack skills, 69, 69*f*; creative competitions activity, 67, 67*f*; creative connections activity, 69, 69*f*; creative poetry activity, 68, 68*f*; drama activities, 65–66, 66*f*; drawing activities, 65, 65*f*; imaginative characters activity, 64, 64*f*; imaginative phonetics and, 63, 63*f*; imaginative word games activity, 64–65, 64*f*; importance of building, 59–63; incidental word learning and, 59; Literacy Bin Activities to build, 63–71; mixing activity types, 20*f*; relationship with comprehension, 60–61; resource materials for building, 66, 66*f*, 71–74; spelling and word close-ups activity, 65, 65*f*; strategy-based instruction for, 46–47, 47*f*; syllabification snap-alongs and, 64, 64*f*; trading cards activity, 66, 66*f*; unique sorting activity, 67, 67*f*; unique word jumbles activity, 67–68, 67*f*; using book-format and graphic organizers, 70, 70*f*; using online websites activity, 66, 66*f*; vocabulary instruction and, 59; Vocabulary Knowledge & Word Skills Rubric, 116*f*, 148; Vocabulary Knowledge & Word Skills Rubric: Writing, 117*f*, 152; word-game-meister activity, 71, 71*f*; word-learning demonstrations, 68, 68*f*

The Vocabulary Book (Graves), 72

The Vocabulary-Enriched Classroom (Block and Mangieri), 72

Vocabulary Instruction (Baumann and Kame'enui), 72

W

Wagner, R.K., 60

water cycle theme, 141

web work activity, 82, 82*f*

websites. *See* online resources

What Really Matters in Fluency (Allington), 102

Wigfield, A., xv, 4

Willingham, D.T., 33, 80

Winograd, P.N., 79

Wisniewski, M., 137

Wood, K.D., 61

word count activities, 101, 101*f*

Word-Game-Meister activity, 71, 71*f*

word games activity, 64–65, 64*f*

word jumbles activity, 67–68, 67*f*

word learning, incidental, 59

word-learning demonstrations, 68, 68*f*

word manipulative activities, 70–71, 70*f*

word skills. *See* vocabulary and word skills

Words, Words, Words (Allen), 72

Y

Yopp, H.K., 59, 60

Yopp, R.H., 59, 60

Z

Zimmermann, S., xii, 41, 42, 56, 78, 87

zoetrope, 49, 49*f*

Zutell, J., 90